Run, Jane, Run...

We Need You In Office!

Maria Rodriguez & Liz Samuel Richards

RUN, JANE, RUN...We Need You in Office!
Why Women Are a Natural for Politics & How to Get More of Them Elected

Copyright © 2018 by Maria Rodriguez & Liz Samuel Richards

Published in the United States by The Leader Is You, Long Grove, IL 60047
runjanerunbook.com
theleaderisyou.com
lizsamuelrichards.com

Cover Design by Rebekah Sather

Photographs for back-cover provided by the authors

Print ISBN: 978-0-9976768-0-8

eBook ISBN: 978-0-9976768-1-5

The quotes that introduce the various sections throughout the book came from a wonderful book that encouraged readers to use them "when they are looking for just the right remark, or need inspiration, advice, or even a bit of humor." We think they have done that and more as they appear throughout this book, and are grateful to Tracy Quinn, the compiling editor, who evidenced a desire to show the strength, compassion, foresight, and wisdom of the women on whose shoulders we currently stand.

Its forward by Cathleen Black is a treasure as well, providing excellent background information about the contributions women have made to both politics and culture. Should you wish to read that background, as well as more of the quotes, we direct you to: *Quotable Women of the Twentieth Century* Edited by Tracy Quinn, with a foreword by Cathleen Black William Morrow and Company, Inc., New York, New York

We have made every effort to give credit and/or attribution to the correct parties. In instances where multiple people or news outlets covered an event or specific story we referenced, credit was given to the particular one that was used as our source.

Our opinions stated throughout the book are our own, based on conclusions we each have drawn over the years from the facts, memories, and events as we saw them, experienced them, or both.

Dedications

From Maria:

To my Aunt Jane, the first "regular" person
I knew who ran for office, and a lifelong example
of humble strength.

From Liz:

To Andrea and to Ron, who kept me afloat
and always believed
I had something worth saying.

And to Amy & The Girls, for whom I said it.

TABLE OF CONTENTS

PART ONE
WOMEN ARE UNIQUELY QUALIFIED AS LEADERS

PART TWO
PUTTING TOGETHER A VIABLE CAMPAIGN

PART THREE
YOU WON – OR LOST – NOW WHAT?

PART FOUR
CLOSING THOUGHTS & RESOURCES

WOMEN ARE UNIQUELY QUALIFIED AS LEADERS

CHAPTER 1

Our Nation's Soul

"Women, if the soul of the nation is to be saved,
I believe that you must become its soul."

Coretta Scott King

Hello! Chances are you have come across this book for one of two reasons. The first is that you have been considering getting into politics in an off-and-on way for some time now, but are not quite sure how to get started, or if you even have what it takes. In that case, this book is for you. It's based on real-life experience, not theory, and will show you the basic ins and outs of what you need to take the political leap with confidence. We can help you realize your potential to effect change!

The second reason you could be looking at this book is because something inside you is saying, "I could do better than those fools running the city," or the state, or even the nation. How many times have you listened to the news and thought, "I really love this country, but right now it's in a pretty big mess." Somewhere in your gut, you know that you, as an intelligent woman, have the common sense, tact, and fairness to take on some of these issues and either solve them or make them more palatable. In fact, you are sure of it. But who are you to speak up and out, you ask yourself. Well, you can stop asking and read this book for some surprising answers.

You are already ahead of most people, because recognizing that they want to help change what they perceive as our country's "mess" is where most people stop. They don't move on to the next step of getting involved. But as you thought about exactly what was wrong, you decided it was incumbent upon *you* to do something. That is where this book comes in. We can help you change things, by helping you take that next step. We believe all women, Millennials, Gen-Xers, and Boomers alike, possess innate leadership skills—they simply hone them through different life experiences. Each group has different strengths, weaknesses, goals and dreams. Some overlap; yet the one thing that remains true for women in all these groups is the possession of those innate skills that they can count on.

Women have been recognized for getting the things done that help companies prosper when they sit on the Board of Directors. Their perspective can change the discussion. Women also have an intuition for risk assessment, even though they may not call it that. Because it is so second nature, they refer to it as simply "the reasons behind my thinking." These skills are not unlike what women do in their heads as mothers. Before answering yes or no to a child's request they quickly determine if the child can handle the implicit risk. It happens so quickly, it just seems *natural* to know how to decide.

The single women who work and do not have families, but have accumulated career expertise, have also honed that skill and multiple others: team player, group leader, mentor, project manager. They, too, could tackle pretty much any problem or task, making the same quick risk management assessments as mothers do. They get daily practice working with cantankerous coworkers, just as mothers corral and manage difficult children.

The Millennials, while highly intelligent, are (strictly by virtue of age) in a bit of a different spot, but no less able to contribute. In most cases, they have not yet built experience either as long-term mothers or long-term career women. But they, too, possess innate skills that can be honed. They are bright, care about the planet, strive to accomplish life balance, and want "to make a difference." They also often have great experience with the latest technology, more than Boomers or even Gen-Xers, making them truly invaluable for making a difference, as we'll see. In addition, they bring an outlook on problem solving that usually leans toward new ways of doing things. And most of them have not yet become jaded.

As we give suggestions, ideas, cautions, and information on how to get elected, we'll address each of these sectors of today's women, because each brings different value to the table—a table which, by the way, has room enough for all.

There is one suggestion that is applicable to all from the very beginning, however; and that is that *we recommend starting with a local office* (library board, city clerk, park commission, etc.) for several reasons:

- It introduces you to the way things work in a government environment. You'll observe other departments in action as well as your own. Soon, you'll have a sense of how things work and the way things fit (and what you think needs to be changed to be either more cost-efficient or productive.)

- It usually costs far less to run for such offices than it does to run for statewide or U.S. Congressional offices.

- You become known, gain name recognition and credibility, and begin to build credentials as a professional. You will then have what's known as "gravitas" and will be taken seriously.

- This is especially true for Millennials; because like it or not, without a certain amount of gravitas acquired through exposure and experience, it will be hard (again, by virtue of your age) for voters to relate to your running as mayor, which would often be the next logical step in our suggested path. So, we suggest you start with one of the abovementioned (or similar) positions, do a good job, and then move up. Establishing that credibility and gravitas is worth the wait!

Most of the women we interviewed for this book not only started at local levels, but rarely saw it as the stepping stone to a larger political career. That larger career grew naturally out of their successes. As Christine Radogno (R) former Illinois Senate Minority Leader who started as Village of LaGrange Trustee, put it when asked how she got into politics:

"For me it was a very local level NIMBY
(Not In My Backyard) issue...a new fire station
would be coming to the end of my street. I knew it
would not be good for a street with napping babies
to have a lot of sirens, and the increased traffic would
not be good for anyone. At the time, I was a stay-at-home
mom who cared about this issue, and I started reading
more about it and going to Board meetings. I was fascinated
by all they did, and how it all worked. How you got stop
signs on corners, how often your garbage would be picked
up and all those other things you take for granted." [1]

Four years later she was running for the Village Board against a "guy who was president of everything." When we asked her how she pulled off a victory, she told us she mobilized all of her resources: networks from schools, church, clubs, and was just very intentional about winning. Never underestimate the incredible resource that is your network. Women are typically masterful networkers, retaining the contacts for years by staying in touch. Larger victories for Radogno followed throughout the years; when she retired in 2017 she had held the office of Minority Leader for eight years. Her story is not all that unusual in the sense that the "awakening" that you want to do something political usually starts with a single issue and grows, often taking your career with it.

You'll find this book blends the wishful with the practical until it becomes the doable. We have facts, theories, and suggestions that will help you decide if you're ready, and for what step and time commitment. Not everyone, especially those with younger families, can afford a full-time involvement; they do, however still want to be involved in improving both their neighborhood's and their country's culture, and there are multiple ways in which they can. Other older women, perhaps with "empty nests," suddenly find themselves with both the time to do more than ever before and the same burning desire to make a difference as their younger

---

1   Christine Radogno. Interview with Maria Rodgriguez, September 28, 2017, Oakbrook
Terrace, Illinois

counterparts. A great example of this was how older and younger women marched side-by-side in the Women's Marches of January 2017.

It's also very important to note that we are addressing women from all political persuasions. Our governmental system depends on the debate of different ideas, whether presented by different political sides or by differing factions within the same side. Throughout, we talk about debate's being the heart of our "process"—and just how important that process is, with the reminder to respect different political ideals or opinions, not demonize each other. The bonus? This book is, in fact, an example of a collaboration from both sides of the aisle. Maria is a registered, though not always in full agreement, Republican and Liz a registered, though not always in full agreement, Democrat. A match made in heaven to foster non-partisanship in the writing.

Both have espoused this "innate skills" theory for years, at the same time living it in their own lives. Like many of you, both started their increasing involvement in community work as volunteers. While Liz's political activities in recent years have often related to the welfare of her marketing clients, she started by being active in her children's school. Maria, while leading first through church and school activities, has gone on to run for and/or hold public office at local, state, and federal levels. Both women started with the desire to reshape either their community, church, schools, or non-profits that they cared about, and graduated to political involvement either as a candidate, a volunteer in support of a candidate, or as a worker for a personally important cause. So, we've been where you are right now, and we *get* you.

Along those same lines, just as we wanted the book to be nonpartisan, we also want the description of the world of politics to be realistic, neither slanted toward the overly optimistic, nor the crushingly pessimistic regarding present day problems or alarming conditions. *As always, somewhere in the middle lies the truth.* Which gives us another truth: some women will be suited to politics naturally—often as an outgrowth of dealing successfully with ornery co-workers, family, or neighbors. They will thrive with the challenges as well as with the simple victories.

Others, however, will have a harder time if elected, and find it less than satisfying to deal with the unpleasantness that sometimes occurs while working toward the solution of a complex problem. But they can still be involved—better suited perhaps for consulting, volunteering, canvassing, or other work that provides invaluable political services to the candidate and party of their choice.

Neither road is wrong; neither road is right as a blanket course for everyone. After reading this book, you will be able to more easily decide for yourself. You will know what is involved, and from your knowledge of yourself, decide which path to take, convinced that you can become an agent of positive change.

Trust us for as long as it takes to read this book, and we promise *you* can be the one stepping forward to make a difference. You can serve as a role model for others, accomplishing things that satisfy your soul and leave a mark on your community, which can lead to opportunities you never dreamed!

CHAPTER 2
Our Basic Premise

"Women are the architects of society."

Harriet Beecher Stowe

The basic premise of this book is that hiding in plain sight are many of the leaders we need. They are the women among us who are mentors, mothers, and nurturers. They are married, single, divorced and widowed. They have the innate skills that have been honed to a level worthy of most any political or corporate office, making them valuable resources in healing our divided nation. Let's take a minute and look at each group individually. Doing so here will give you a sense of the strong shoulders on which you stand, and the legacy of women that is already in place. It will give you added confidence as you begin to take your place among those who make a difference.

Mothers

Mothering, for instance, requires relentless management decisions, including NASA-worthy logistics. But logistics is only one of a mother's basic skills. If you have been a mother or a nurturing mentor, you have most likely been asked to volunteer (on multiple occasions) by school, church or community. You've run events, being fully responsible for profit and loss, which means you employed strategic planning to maximize attendance, accurate price setting to maximize both sales and profit, human resource skills to placate "competing" volunteers, and crisis management at its highest level when the band that was going to play at your dinner dance got snowed in at an airport somewhere.

Complying with those many volunteer requests you put those skills to further and extended use, honing them as you went. When we hear the argument that we should vote for political candidates who are successful business people, we argue that mothering may be a better training ground! Why? Because mothering takes into account all the stakeholders, not just the bottom line. Since you can't fire you family, you naturally learn to deal with people in the most productive way.

So don't doubt yourself—the leader is you! See yourself as one. Conduct yourself as a person of power and influence. You are fully equipped and have more impact than you know. History has shown that female influence is significant and necessary to building whole and balanced societies. We have many examples of just such women throughout this book. We urge you to follow in their footsteps—and will show you how.

And as for the young mother who, though she wants to make a difference, feels the time crunch of raising her family and can't imagine fitting any more into her already packed life, we can show you how to grow your influence by simply seeing yourself through a different lens (that of leadership) and carrying yourself accordingly. We all can make a difference with every life we touch.

For the mother of children approaching adulthood who has enjoyed raising them and wonders if life will feel empty as her children become adults, this book will definitely strike a chord. We need your wisdom and informed authoritative voice to help rebalance our culture. Take the skills you have honed and step into a new arena where you are sorely needed. This includes any woman who has never had children of her own, but has filled or supplemented such a role along her way. Favorite aunts, godmothers, next-door neighbors, big sisters...you are invaluable.

When we say we need you, or that you are invaluable, it is not just a line in a paragraph to get your attention. We are very concerned about the leadership crisis that currently exists in this country, and the self-interest-only attitude that is evident at just about every level. We desperately need leaders who can see all sides of situations. We need mothers! It's not the first time that mothers or mother figures were needed to "heal." In fact, our first example is that of Mother's Day itself, founded by Anna Jarvis in 1905.

History books tell us Jarvis wanted to recognize her recently deceased mother for her incredible contributions healing the nation following the Civil War. Her mother, Ann Reeves Jarvis was a peace activist who cared for wounded soldiers and established "Mother's Day Work Clubs" to address public health issues. In caring for soldiers from **both** the Union and the Confederacy, she put forth one of the first "across the aisle" efforts, leading by example. She likely had personal feelings about one side or the other, but she could keep those opinions in perspective and help heal the nation through her unbiased healing of its people from both North and South. Women through the centuries have seemed especially gifted with the demeanor needed to do this. We are healers.

The Single Women

Another example of women's ability to see the big picture and recognize the value of each element of the whole, is to look at Florence Nightingale. She saw the big picture during the Crimean War.[2] The British lost roughly 23,000 men—but amazingly, only 4,000 had been wounded! The overwhelming majority died of rampant disease, a result of the leaders' not seeing the full picture. If they had, they would have, like Nightingale, recognized that patient care would begin by providing sanitary conditions and isolating soldiers who are contagious. Those two caveats would become the hallmarks of effective field treatment.

Nightingale's recognition of this need for care of the wounded set the stage for future war contingencies that were put in place. Ironically,

---

2   Christopher J. and Gillian C. Gill. *Nightengale in Scutari: Her Legacy Reexamined.* Center for International health, Boston University School of Public Health, Boston, MA, Review Article. June 2005. http://docplayer.net/7218163-Nightingale-in-scutari-her-legacy-reexamined.html Accessed June 20, 2018.

it would be many, many years before any of the wartime surgeons themselves were women.

Today, of course, we recognize that so many of our current and "routine" medical procedures had their start as inventions born from necessity in what were eventually established field hospitals and MASH (Mobile Army Surgical Hospital) units. As we would see time and time again, it was a woman who was at the forefront of something big enough to change our culture for the better.

Other stories abound where individual women play prominent leadership roles. Joan of Arc comes to mind and we encourage you to learn her full story. Legend has it that she was a respected leader, and men much older than her seventeen years willingly followed her into battle. Knowing her as a fierce warrior, once the battle was finally over they watched in undisguised admiration as she comforted the dying on both sides.

Today we are here again, at a time in history where we need such true leadership as these women provided. A leadership that stirs the soul of all those who can't, on their own, see a forward path. While it's true that mothers supply this kind of leadership every day to their own families, so do single female mentors and single female relatives, friends, and co-workers. Women from all walks of life are blazing trails and writing books to pass on the knowledge gleaned, such as those we will mention and others you will find in our Reference Section in Part Four. They could share that knowledge even further by running for office, in their own communities, moving on to higher races if they so choose.

In the workplace, women both married and single have shattered a number of glass ceilings. However, many such ceilings still remain. But each shattering represents growth. There are some statistics of how we lag behind other countries in this area, but we don't need statistics to see it's true. We only have to see our lesser percentage of a dollar's pay, in some cases still as low as fifty-six cents (for Latina women) compared to a man's earned dollar. [3]

Myths about women being "ditzy" were pretty much dispelled over fifty years ago. But, that does not mean that anything resembling reality as to their strengths and capabilities has supplanted those myths in any but a few quarters. In addition, the unfortunate pitting of working women against stay-at-home moms, has left many women with doubts as to their priorities and choices, and even in some cases, as to their capabilities.

This is one trend that we both think needs to be eradicated. In our minds, the true definition of feminism is choosing a life path that challenges you and leaves you fulfilled, and not being judged for that choice once it has been made. It is not whether you work or stay home; it is whether you are free to do either. As former First Lady Betty Ford said, "A liberated woman is one who feels confident in herself and is happy with what she is doing. She is a person who has a sense of self…" [4]

So enough already! We need to respect one another for the part that each plays in the greater whole that is womanhood. Some women work outside the home, through either choice or financial necessity. They provide the female perspective that offers added dimension in the business world. Women who choose to stay home, in addition to running their own homes, are often the volunteers running different organizations that enrich all our lives. These volunteer efforts keep the costs down by literally millions of dollars and help provide services that would otherwise not be available. In a nutshell, we believe that we should see it this way (our words):

Women, whether they spend their time working inside or outside the home are blessed with innate leadership skills. Since these are so often associated with mothering (leading

---

3   Ariane Hegewisch, M.Phil., Emma Williams-Baron. *The Gender Wage Gap: 2017 Earnings Differences by Race and Ethnicity* March 7, 2018 (Source: The Institute for Women's Policy Research) https://iwpr.org/publications/gender-wage-gap-2017-race-ethnicity/ Accessed June 20, 2018.

4   *Quotable Women of the Twentieth Century*, Edited by Tracy Quinn. 1999, William Morrow and Co., Inc., New York, New York

a child into adulthood), they are not generally grouped with "management" skills. As a result, with no thought to the executive-quality traits they represent, they lose the patina of pure leadership by being classified as "mothering" or "nurturing" skills.

Ironically, women's innate leadership skills, which we go into more fully a bit later, are the very same skills that are in demand all over the business and political world as this is being written. More frequent use of these "soft" skills would mean less need for the more aggressive and more destructive ones. It would also eliminate some of the aggressive posturing we find so common in the world today.

Of note, these specific leadership skills are present in women every-where—culture, race, and era notwithstanding. They are universally (though we are not saying exclusively) ours. They enable us to move seamlessly between the many roles we assume each day. They are also transferable and translatable into the business and political worlds beyond. They transfer from teaching children not to play in the street to risk man-agement in corporations; from teaching standing up for yourself, to cour-age on a world stage against aggression; from teaching children to do the right thing even when nobody is watching, to having politicians embrace a code of ethics that stands the test of observation and not simply conve-nience. Thus, they are quantifiable as productive, effective, and scalable… business hallmarks, all.

We guarantee these positive character traits and leadership skills are inside you—and we want very much to help you recognize them in your-self as well as in other women. They will take you places.

How That Works

Let's examine this phenomenon a bit. The reason that the human race is still on the planet is because women have babies. And one thing is certain; no matter the conditions of parentage, a baby left on a street corner to fend for itself cannot survive either physically or emotionally. A mother, or a mother figure, is needed. The U.S. Census Bureau put out a press release in Feb. of 2016 which said there are 43.5 million women between the ages of fifteen and fifty who have given birth to 95.8 million children.[5] That's a lot of children who need mothers. Fortunately, that's also a lot of mothers. We recognize that not all mothers or mother figures are going to provide everything needed physically and emotionally for their children, but most at least try. And as they do, they come to care about things *in their child's world* that they didn't even give thought to before.

When they see the state of our culture, with its disrespect for fellow human beings, violence, and a simple lack of civility, it makes their jobs as mothers or mother figures quite complex. They need to teach their children how to navigate this world; and there is no handbook. Mothers rely on their internal moral compasses and natural instincts, usually inherited from and nurtured by their own mothers, aunts or grandmothers. Those were the women who told them what's right or wrong, what is acceptable, and what is doable through effort and perseverance. **(Please don't send us letters. We realize that there are fine male role models as well—but that's a different book.)** Mothers and mentors do their best to lead by example, even when facing doubt or fear. We think the venerable Helen Hayes said it quite simply, but quite profoundly:

> *"Yes, I have doubted, I have wandered off the path, but I always return. It is intuitive, an intrinsic, built-in sense of direction. I seem to always find my way home…"* [6]

Mothers and their stand-ins probably succeed more times than not in raising healthy, well-adjusted children who grow to adults and contribute positively to society. That's no accident. *And these leadership talents don't "age out" of the women's daily lives as their children do!* When children are grown, and move out as adults, they don't take their mother's skills with them. They leave her with hers and take as their own the many lessons which she (their favorite and most inspirational leader) has passed

5   U.S. Census Bureau, Press Release April 20, 2016. (Release Number: CB16-FF.09 *UPDATED8) Current Population Survey 2014. https://www.census.gov/newsroom/facts-for-features/2016/cb16-ff09.html Accessed June 20, 2018.

6   Quinn, *Quotations*, page 85

on to them by her example. And the cycle repeats itself, passing not just to any children of their own, but also to friends, colleagues, and the entire circle of the grown child's influence.

So, let's say you're a mom, and your children are still young; but you picked up this book because you want to make a difference. However, you know you can't give it quite your "all" because the kids still need your time and involvement. You're in the same boat as a professional woman whose job takes her full day. Let's explore what you CAN do both professionally and/or in your home with traits that you may have overlooked. We already discussed logistics as the getting of people and materials from here to there, and perhaps back again. In addition to logistics, there are, in no particular order:

- ORGANIZATION
- PRIORITY SETTING
- SUPERVISION
- COACHING
- TEAMWORK
- CONFLICT RESOLUTION
- PREVENTIVE MAINTENANCE
- PROJECT MANAGEMENT
- FUNDRAISING
- PRODUCT DEVELOPMENT

Obviously, not all people will rise to the highest levels of competency and performance with their transferable skills, but they *will* be able to transfer them. Suddenly you are aware that you are good at going from short- and long-term planning to logistics, and from individual coaching to developing teamwork. You pull various committees together as part of project management, and think outside the box in project development. If you don't think you have all the above, try creating your skills resume. Many women are astonished to find that they use these skills both naturally and continually. Any skills that they don't currently have can be acquired! Women find new strengths every day.

Don't put this off. It's definitely both enlightening and worth your while to actually sit down and write a skills resume. Think back from (or ahead to) the moment you left your parents' house to strike out on your own. Again, this is not a resume of paying jobs, but a resume of valuable skills.

For instance, when you moved into your first apartment and decided what to keep and what to pitch; what needed to be easily available because it would be used most often; where to put the television for best light conditions and audio, you began to fully explore *and exercise* the innate skill muscles. Write those early tasks down on one side of a sheet of paper and across from each one write the skills involved: organization, planning, or priority setting, for example.

If you have decided on dating some people and rejecting others, you made discernments as to values compatible with your own. The same would be true in the selection of political parties. You began to look beneath the surface and see what feels right to you, trusting one of your most valuable assets, your instinct. Oprah thinks so highly of instinct that she has said on her show, "Follow your instincts. That's where true wisdom manifests itself." [7]

Next, if you married and planned your wedding, write the steps down across from those enormous tasks: budgeting, sourcing, logistics, people-skill tasks like thank-you notes and table assignments (you're using human resources, event planning, communication skills, etc.). Did you have to integrate yourself(selves) into a new neighborhood, or find a church? Joining the neighborhood watch patrol is risk management, finding the right church/restaurants/gym is research.

Get the idea? We guarantee that if you start doing this, even if you have never yet held a paying job, or never plan to, you will be ready to show skillset availability. Your self-esteem will skyrocket; and you will feel capable of anything! The best part is, your life will not stay stagnant;

---

7 Quinn, *Quotations*, page 12

neither will your skills. They will grow to meet your increased confidence to take on new responsibilities.

You will even, in some cases, be able to quantify your skills with numbers that are impressive. For example, "Sent a letter to parents that resulted in immediate 15% increase in PTO membership, with attendant increase in funds through dues, and in volunteerism due to additional available members."

You may say men have these skills too. And you would be right. This is most definitely not a book about man bashing. But let's look at a key difference. Women turn to these skills on a daily basis, and they do so *instinctively*. While some men may also do that, a good number *LEARN* them either in management courses in business school or while in corporate management trainee programs, neither of which, until recent decades, women had access to in any great numbers. Yet, since the beginning, women have demonstrated these skills regardless of education, wealth, or management training. Even women in the poorest nations, with no schooling at all, stepped up using their natural abilities. Lest we forget, male leaders usually *began* their leadership path by learning from their "leader" mothers.

CHAPTER 3

Turning Skills Into Action

"Life shrinks or expands in proportion to one's courage."

Anais Nin

So, back to our former scenario: you have these skills, and you want to make a difference, but you have limited time available. Or, you don't know where to begin because it's the first time you have given this any real thought. What's the first step? It starts with a decision to begin right now, from right where you are. Then the mental toughness begins to grow as you start and then continue to see yourself through the leadership lens. As we said earlier, don't doubt yourself. See yourself as an influential leader and conduct yourself as a person of power. You can do this. Here are some specific steps, expanded upon from their earlier mention:

Start small, with your local community or other sphere of interest and volunteer.

Maria started as a volunteer for the village clerk, a role requiring two evenings out per month. She then went on to be Village Trustee, and later to serve as Village President. Her whole political career was *rooted* in volunteerism. If you have been a volunteer in the past, you are already more prepared than you think. Here are a few ideas where you can "explore" your preferences and opportunities by beginning as a volunteer, then moving higher if you wish. Remaining a volunteer, with all the incredible value they provide, is also an option:

- **Library** –Volunteer for a while, then eventually run for a seat on the Library Board. Meetings take maybe one night per month.

- **Your village** – See what volunteer positions are open and take advantage of the hands-on learning they will provide.

- **School** – Don't just help with the book fair or other PTO tasks; work to increase membership. Put yourself in a position where you can bring up issues and help effect change. Then run for an office such as secretary, treasurer, or even president.

- **Church** – If you're musical, organize a choir if there isn't one. Set up babysitting programs for Sunday services. This is especially important to a church that is small and has few paid staff on board. Then look into what's open in the way of participation in the Parish Council or on the Finance Committee. If you can balance a checkbook and run your family's finances, just think of this as a "bigger" family—your church family! Churches offer a volunteer opportunity for any personality; join something that interests you. Then, as time permits, offer to step up as chairman. This public service is a GREAT training ground for politics...trust us.

- **School Board** –There are a couple of different options here. Catholic schools often have a School Board made up of parishioners who oversee the school. Charter schools have a School Board responsible for interpreting the charter. There is also, of course, the traditional public School Board in your local district. Go to the meetings at least a couple of times; check out what area of discussion/concern appeals to you. Maybe ask one of the elected Board members to grab a cup of coffee and give you some insight as to what the time involvement and pertinent issues are.

- **City Council or Village Board** – Meetings are typically once or twice a month. The time commitment depends on the size of your community and the goals of the sitting Board. Again, get to know the current members and attend some meetings. It's good information as to how different offices work within the whole, even if you decide this particular route isn't for you.

- **Township Office** – Your township offers services that add to your quality of life more than you know—especially if there are parts of your town that are unincorporated. Go to the meetings and check out how services are grouped and organized. There may be an area that needs a chairman, or will in a year when the current one retires. It may even present the chance to champion something you already have great interest in or concern about.

Township government is also a great area for those with environmental interests. In our fast-paced world, pulling back from technology and enhancing the natural landscape can be incredibly rewarding for both our own and future generations. It can also be a useful training ground for those who wish to move on to larger environmental issues. You never know where it will take you. Rachel Carson and her groundbreaking book *Silent Spring* comes to mind. The book, showing the harm that certain pesticides caused, was so well documented that the government banned DDT for agricultural use in spite of the conflicting information presented by the chemical industry,

Neither one of us is trying to turn this into a treatise on environmentalism. We are, rather, using the subject to show that it is usually the women who dare to light the flame of knowledge and change; and it is the women who keep it burning.

- **County Board** – This is usually where the more seasoned political minds in your area can be found. The decisions made here directly affect your life; so get to know what this area of government is all about. These positions are typically more time consuming, because they control both structure and funding of accomplishing everything from zoning to liquor licenses, to the many school districts' funding and accountability. For the Board, either volunteer experience or political experience is helpful. County Board positions often pay a salary, or at least a stipend.

- **Volunteer for a candidate whose principles you believe in** and help him or her get elected. You will wear many hats and learn firsthand what makes a campaign succeed or fail. Very valuable information and experience to have—especially if you yourself ever decide to run for office.

- **Volunteer for your local already-elected ("sitting") representative** if you think politics is definitely for you. Learn it from the ground up, which is the best way to fully understand the process. Since their budgets are never enough to accommodate all the needs and services they would like to provide to constituents, they can use all the volunteer hours they can get. Call their office and find out what help they need. And once you are welcomed into the fold, don't be afraid to ask questions! Politicians love to talk about their work, and you will learn a lot.

The same advice about volunteering holds true for single women as well as married women without children. It's an excellent way to start your political explorations—but without the demands of young children, you have other options as well. One of them would be to run for a full-time office in an area you particularly want to affect. Again, start locally. Learn; establish yourself; and work your way up so you are seen as (and are) an experienced candidate.

Brush up on your mentoring skills. At its core politics is about getting everyone on board and working toward the same goal. If you don't hold a job that presents opportunities for mentoring, then you may want to volunteer for a mentoring organization such as the Big Brother/Big Sister program. Those roles not only hone your innate skills, but also prepare you for the exciting and unpredictable world of politics.

Now, having given you some basic ideas of why you have the skills you need, and the potential to leverage them, let's explore how to get elected to those leadership positions. We won't be telling you how to run a campaign specific to your office or geographic area because we don't know either your particular choice of office, or your available resources. But, we will be telling you the basics of running *any* good campaign. You can adapt the suggestions as needed to fit your specifics. But remember, one basic rule that never changes is to be sure you are prepared by knowing what the office entails—and having conviction that you can do it. As we transition into that, let us leave you with two more quotes from women:

> *"We must not, in trying to think about how we can make a difference, ignore the small daily differences we can make which, over time, add up to big differences that we often cannot foresee."*
>
> Marian Wright Edelman[8]

> *"It's never too late to become what you might have been."*
>
> George Eliot (a.k.a. Mary Ann Evans)[9]

---

8   Quinn, Quotations, page 6.

9   George Eliot Quotes. BrainyQuote.com, Xplore Inc., 28. https://www.brainyquote. com/quotes/george_eliot_161679, Accessed April 23,2018.

CHAPTER 4

Where Are We Right Now?

*"The stakes are too high for government
to be a spectator sport."*

Barbara Jordan

If true that animals sense shifts in the earth that signal oncoming storms and powerful winds, they must have had a field day in 2016. More than one person of note has pointed out that not since 1968, that "other" milestone year in our country's history, have Americans witnessed such a clash of cultures, upending of the status quo, and rising up of an electorate determined to be heard, valued, and respected.

The unprecedented rise of Donald Trump, the fall of Hillary Clinton, and an almost successful takeover of the Democratic party by a grandfatherly senator from Vermont mimicked those turbulent days from a generation ago almost to a tee. The grandfather from those days, Gene McCarthy, who at that time mobilized grass roots movements of those feeling disenfranchised, also won a surprisingly threatening number of votes. Similarities to then and now are actually pretty eerie in a good number of ways. There are some excellent books included in the Reference Section of Part Four that will astound you as to how we are repeating history. We urge you to read at least one.

You will see that we were, at that time engaged in a war far away that had gone on too long with no traditional victory in sight. Voter rights were a huge issue, especially in the south. Equal civil rights for all

Americans, especially people of color, were center stage for affordable housing and integrated neighborhoods and schools; equal opportunity to apply for and get jobs; and the right to eat in the same restaurants, use the same restrooms, and drink from the same water fountains as white citizens. The establishment was being challenged, especially by college-aged students who were not busy fighting overseas (resulting in the often-recited evaluation of Vietnam as a "poor man's war" since those who did not have college deferments were drafted, and often killed in disproportionate numbers to the general population.) Hollywood was far-left liberal; drugs were being introduced as opening the way to a new culture; the land was being raped by unscrupulous developers and "dumpers" and the water in the lakes and rivers was becoming polluted. Family dinners could easily become opportunities for further disparaging "draft dodgers" who fled to Canada, boys with long hair, and the evils of "dissing" the government and its leaders. Women realized they deserved a place at the corporate and political tables, and began fighting for them with demonstrations and advocacy for equal opportunity. In other words, in these ways and many others, with due respect to the scientific, medical, and social breakthroughs, after a whole generation we're back where we started.

We think it's fair (meaning both your Republican author Maria and your Democratic author Liz would agree) that the country has not since then been as polarized as it is now. That's why this book is, as we said, as non-partisan as we can possibly make it, because our topic transcends such narrow "party" labels. We think it's also fair to say that Donald Trump did the country a huge favor by running. Why? Because it feels like everyone on the planet has suddenly, with his election, realized that politics indeed affects us all, for better or worse, depending on your point of view.

Our government was meant to be a representative government, meaning that each of us is entitled to a voice that can be heard by the elected officials. Seldom has articulating that voice been so apparent, and so much on the minds of the everyday man or woman. Good and thoughtful people who may have never taken the time to do so before, are looking at government through newly opened eyes. Today you will find yourself able to have a political conversation (though maybe not a pleasant or insightful one) with almost anyone. People are discussing issues again, and not just giving them lip service. And what they are forced to face and take a stand on is worrying them—no matter what side of the aisle they call home.

It was within this framework that women were so forcefully included in the 2016 election—as presidential candidate on one end of the evolution spectrum, and as the target of sexual jokes, disrespectful remarks, and teenaged-level attention to prettiness on the opposite less evolved end. Something had to give. And it did! Women rose up—en masse—as did many other groups that also felt disrespected or ignored. And at the forefront of almost all of those groups were the women.

We are certainly not the only two people to have noticed these things. Issues in politics are now at what both of your authors feel is "critical mass." Something is in the air, and it does have to do with women. We have a chance right now, as women leaders had before us, to make a huge difference by our active participation. We have a chance to prove as women, through our actions and accomplishments, that we are up to any task which includes getting involved in cultural or governmental issues. This goes beyond marches, though marches are a start and certainly help you make a statement. *But getting elected helps you make laws. And laws determine society's boundaries.*

We mentioned earlier, and stress again here, that history shows that the female impact is significant and necessary to building whole and balanced societies. That's why earlier we used Harriet Beecher Stowe's quote from many years ago, "Women are the architects of society" when we stated the premise of our book. True then; true now. We should need no greater motivation for involvement.

History also clearly shows that lack of balance evidences itself in such massive unrest and "rising up" as we saw in 1968 and are seeing again now. Such rising up is never, however, about just one thing or one issue. That certainly proved to be true in the 1968 election when the protestors who came to Chicago came from the anti-war movement, the peace movement (yes, they were different), the women's movement, the civil rights and voting rights movements, as well as several student political movements such as SDS (Students for a Democratic Society). Perfect example of "not just one thing."

Recent election debates have shown the tremendous breadth of issues on voters' minds, thereby drawing even more demographics into the political discussion than usual, many for the first time. That's why it's "go big or go home" in the sense of needing involvement from those who care.

If you're reading this book, you obviously care. Now it's your turn! Start by listening to the news on various channels–those that both do and don't support your own political view. Read various op-ed pieces and blogs to sort out in your own head who the players are at any level of office, what they stand for, and what their responsibilities are. Then you can tell if they are fulfilling them or not; or if they are, but not to your satisfaction.

The controversial issues are complicated. There are never simple answers—if there were, they would all be solved by now. Education, healthcare, immigration, to name a few, all deserve to be broken down into smaller issues, discussed as such, and then re-incorporated to develop legislation that is palatable to most, if not the majority. Pro-free trade or pro-nationalism, pro-public education or pro-charter schools and vouchers, pro-tax reduction or pro-government spending—and on and on, issue after issue. The same is true for local as well as national problems.

So, in true American fashion, discussions continue around dinner tables in small towns and large, in barber shops and on evening trains and buses. Friendships have ended over less. And as during the Civil War, or more recently, during Vietnam, families are often divided by the stand taken brother against brother, father against child, husband against wife. Practically nobody has escaped having to stand toe-to-toe with someone important in their lives over at least one hot-button issue.

Well-known newswoman and writer Cokie Roberts was recently on a news show discussing how the polarizing atmosphere we have now reminds her of her family's Thanksgiving dinners during the Vietnam era. During those, she said, the family "rule" was to keep the conversation around what your dog was doing…it was the only safe conversation to have! Or to translate for our purposes, the only issue with a single side.

For many who dreamed of going back to "normal" after the 2016 election, normal no longer exists. Where are the cool heads that prevail? Where are the people who can restore order out of chaos? Where are the people who have a moral compass and an ability to persist until the job is done? *In other words, where are the women?*

CHAPTER 5

Where Are the Women?

"Women have always been the guardians of wisdom and humanity, which makes them natural but usually secret rulers. The time has come for them to rule openly, but together with and not against men."

Charlotte Wolff

Women hold the key and are hiding in plain sight. But as so often happens when people get mired in fear and negativity, solutions (and the people who hold them) go unnoticed. Women need to be noticed now more than ever, while the country comes to grips with the fact that not only have our politics been skewed away from historical benchmarks and traditions, so has our culture. A lack of civility has replaced manners, and instead of demanding better from our politicians, we have settled for less—much less. All of us. And we are paying a price in every political and cultural area.

Women, though, tend to look at history and see a bigger picture. These are not our darkest days. Imagine the polarization after the Civil War. That was unprecedented, yet we pulled out of it, grew, and prospered. Women knew how to lead such efforts, and in many cases, it was (and is) by recognizing the price we are paying in those political and cultural areas—and stepping up to say it's time for a change.

Our aim is to show how women, specifically, can address the state of the country, and help move it forward in a positive direction. That means, regardless of any personal feelings on an issue, we urge you to take no party's side, leaving yourself free to explore all ideas, solutions and recommendations that may be relevant. This is why women are a natural for politics. We actually think differently than men, with the important point being that our brains focus more on conciliatory activity.

A 2013 study has shown,[10] through monitoring actual brain activity, that women indeed *do* think differently than men, using different parts of their brains to solve problems. Our own folklore, and books such as John Gray's bestselling *Men Are from Mars, Women Are from Venus*, have previously attested to this with anecdotal evidence. Nonetheless, it's good to know our thesis is definitely supported by science that says women are relying more heavily on those parts that most assist in unifying, calming, mediating, and compromising, taking a measured approach to issues.

If ever there were a need for a unifying, calming, and taking a measured approach to the issues, it is now! If ever there were a need for those prepared to mediate, reconcile and compromise it is now! *Which means, if ever there were an overwhelming need for women to step up and enter the political arena, it is now!* Using the characteristics just mentioned, as well as others, we are uniquely and profoundly qualified to lead.

If you don't know whether to accept that last statement at face value, consider this: in 2013, during the government shutdown when the entire government was closed, including the national parks, and the men stood about blustering to each other, it was the *women* of the Senate, the *women* on the Hill, who came together, said "Enough is enough," and did something about it. They took charge. They put together the necessary proposals, compromises, and agendas to get the gears of national government unstuck and moving again. Most importantly, they did it in days, not months; and they did it without raging animosity (or hormones) or partisan roadblocks. In effect, they called on their well-honed "family management" skills and sent the children to their rooms while they, the adults, figured out how to fix the mess we were ALL in.

---

10   Tanya Lewis. *How Men's Brains Are Wired Differently than Women's.* Live Science, Scientific American. December 2, 2013 https://www.scientificamerican.com/article/how-mens-brains-are-wired-differently-than-women/ Accessed June 20, 2018.

And we love the way they did it! According to a *Time* magazine piece by Jay Newton Small on Oct. 16, 2013 in *swampland.time* (*Time*'s online political section) called *Women Are the Only Adults Left in Washington* and later in *Time* Magazine's print issue of October 28, 2013, titled *The Last Politicians*, the author clearly demonstrates why women are so uniquely qualified to step up in politics. Here's what happened, for those of you that do not recall.[11]

It started with Republican Senator Susan Collins of Maine stepping up on the Senate floor on October 8 (when the situation regarding the shutdown was perhaps at its worst) and proposing a plan: "I ask my Democratic and Republican colleagues to come together. We can do it. We can legislate responsibly and in good faith."

In response, Senate Appropriations chair Barbara Mikulski, (D) Maryland, said "Let's get to it. Let's get the job done. I am willing to negotiate. I am willing to compromise." And so it went. In a matter of minutes, they were joined by Alaska Republican Lisa Murkowski. What most Americans didn't know was that the night before, a majority of the Senate's twenty women members gathered for pizza in New Hampshire's Democratic Senator Jeanne Shaheen's office, and the discussion centered around Collins' plan to reopen the government. How? With some simple basic compromises. Joining the aforementioned women were Minnesota Democrat Amy Klobuchar who, according to Small, proposed adding the repeal of the medical-device tax. Senate Agriculture chair Debbie Stabenow (D) Michigan, offered the pulling of revenue from her stalled farm bill. And so it went.

The women legislators worked in an atmosphere of mutual personal respect and support, give and take, and shared responsibility. After several hours, they were joined by more senators, including a couple of men (Small doesn't name the men). Together they ate their pizza and their salads, drank their wine, and came up with a plan that all could live with. It

---

11   Jay Newton-Small. *Women Are the Only Adults Left in Washington.* Swampland, Time. October 16, 2013. (later seen in Time Magazine's October 28, 2013 print issue, re-titled *The Last Politicians*.) http://swampland.time.com/2013/10/16/women-are-the-only-adults-left-in-washington/ *Accessed June 20, 2018.*

extended the debt ceiling, which reopened the government, and the compromises regarding the bills and Obamacare represented a true bipartisan effort.

In the rest of the article, Small talks about the distinct differences in the women's behaviors and customs vs. the men's. It is the same type code of ethics that we have been advocating, simply said in different words. Here, in our opinion, are a few of the key points:

- Civility above all else is the rule.

- They censor each other should that rule break down.

- Support beats competition when trying to accomplish things.

- Support results in compromise.

- They are women confident enough to keep their female side alive, giving bridal and baby showers, having mentoring sessions and luncheons. For example, Dianne Feinstein(D) California, makes herself available to any new Senator to share the basics of the office.

- All twenty female Senators (four Republicans and sixteen Democrats) continually act as drivers of legislation, responsible for the majority of legislation passed last year.

- They chair or rank on ten of the twenty Senate committees.

- They play on sports teams after they change from pearls and stockings and skirts of a certain length (Senator Feinstein's dress code for her staff, minus the pearls. Those are *her* trademark.)

- They remind each other that they are speaking for all American women in their tackling of "women's" issues.

These things are the intangibles that make women politicians successful. And it shows in daily conduct and success, not just in this one instance, however notable this instance may be. Small calls the shutdown example a "lab test" of sorts that can finally prove empirically what women already know: "that when you put women in power positions they function differently from men, more collaboratively and thus more effectively. As Senator Heidi Heitkamp (D) North Dakota put it to Small:

"One of the things we do a bit better is listen. It is about getting people in a room with different life experiences who will look at things a little differently because they're moms, because they're daughters who've been taking care of senior moms, because they have a different life experience than a lot of senior guys in the room." [12]

Even these senators, however, still face challenges; but our money's on them! They were uniquely qualified because they understood the system and combined that knowledge with the traits that are innate to women: listening, asking questions to reach the bigger picture, learning from past experiences and mistakes, and guiding the less-skilled among them without demagoguery or derision.

Liz's favorite line in the Small article was the very last one, a quote from Senator John McCain of Arizona, "…Imagine what they could do if there were fifty of them."

Paraphrasing, Senator Heitkamp pointed out that in many cases those skills were honed as they ran households and simultaneously held volunteer posts in schools, churches, and communities. Others in that group who are single transferred those same skills they saw in their own childhood homes, learned in school, then honed over the years in corporate offices and non-profit organizations. Each group produced leaders. Over the years, each group learned how to:

- cooperate
- support each other
- find funding for projects
- make schools (or work organizations) better
- make churches more relevant
- make communities more welcoming
- make resources more protected, and safer for man and his environment.

---

12   Ibid, citing Senator Heidi Heitkamp

And the final unifying factor is this: they are all saying enough is enough! Have you reached *your* "Enough is enough" moment? Is that why you are reading this book? Do you have ideas, even if only in formative stages, of how to make things better? Then consider running for office, at whatever level you think suits you now—local, state or federal. Make a difference.

You are fully equipped to make that difference. Maria has the real-life experience in the political arena to see that statement acted out over and over again.

She can help you to have a deeper understanding of our governmental process, why it is extraordinary, and why it is most definitely worth fighting to preserve. Let's listen to her in her own words for a bit.

"As mayor, I was the chief executive of a town (actually, a village) which allowed me to see how the jobs and responsibilities of different areas of government functioned together as a whole. I didn't just have 'my' job to focus on in a vacuum.

"It was during that time that I discovered the leadership traits I had taken for granted. They had fully developed and sharpened over the years through mentoring and then mothering. Until assuming the office of mayor, I had never really thought of mothering as both a training ground and proving ground for leadership skills. But let me tell you what I learned.

"When I was elected, I met with the Village Manager who would be the staff member directly reporting to me. His name was Dave Lothspeich. He proved himself to be a great asset—reliable and always ethical. We laughed about our first meeting for years afterward. In typical "newcomer" fashion, I told him that I was "goal oriented" and ready to "move things forward." He respectfully told me that the *process* was as important as the goal. I eventually became a reluctant believer, and respecting the process changed the way I look at politics. It still influences the criteria for how I vote. I make sure that people I vote for will respect the process as well. Otherwise, my vote is going elsewhere."

Let's talk about "the process," which consists of the steps that are taken to make progress on an issue by the governing body in control of its outcome, usually through voting. (That means things go from an idea for a law formed in the relevant committee, to the floor to be debated, followed by a vote of the members as to either "yea" or "nay.") The majority leader of the body, such as the Senate, or even some large city councils, is in charge of scheduling the bill for floor debate and vote. Not *all* bills, however, are guaranteed to make it out of committee and onto the floor for debate. The committee is supposed to serve as the initial vetting for any bill.

Another way to look at "the process" in politics is to compare the politician's successes in their executive positions such as mayor or governor to the business person's success in the C-Suite (CEO, COO, CFO, CMO, etc.) We feel those two processes and skillsets are very different.

For instance, it is possible that a successful business person will have the needed skills to also be successful in government, but not always. Not understanding the inherent "institutional" differences between corporate leadership and political leadership can make or break an administration. When you are the owner or CEO in business, you lay out your vision and typically fire anyone who is underperforming, even if you have a Board of Directors to go through.

In contrast, in the Executive offices of the government, you lay out your vision during the campaign, and you are voted in as the voice of those who elected you. One of the first hurdles you may encounter is that *you cannot fire any underperforming legislators, even those intentionally working to undermine your progress, because they also were elected. You have to be able to work with everyone to build consensus.* When you start at the local level, by the time you decide to run for a higher executive government position, you will be well versed in how to build consensus.

Another important point: the executive office in government is not supposed to be a voting position. The job of the President, Governor, or Mayor is to facilitate the good (read respectful and productive) debate. Such debate is fundamental to our governmental system. It is actually *required* to enact good laws. Following this sometimes-arduous process ensures fewer unintended consequences that would render the law potentially harmful to certain groups or individuals. Well written legislation rarely needs to be overturned. The great Presidents from both sides of the aisle have all had this in common: they could respect the individual even if they didn't agree with his or her politics; and they could have a discussion with the goal of finding an answer rather than proving their own theory.

Again, we see the parallels to motherhood. As a mother, you lay out the general expectation and then work within house rules, with all the quirky personalities both inside and outside of your family, finally arriving at solutions or policies everyone can live with, even if they don't totally agree.

I believe that is why, as mayor, I felt so comfortable in drawing personalities with opposing views to the table in search of a common goal. I saw the first key to governing as respect, which forces us to focus on issues, not people and personalities.

And I saw the second key as respect for ourselves, and the wisdom and skills we possess. When you respect yourself, others respect you. That's why we are stressing again and again that these skills are already inside you—because unfortunately, we often have no faith in ourselves as a leader or agent of change. Cynthia Heimel said it better than perhaps anyone when she said comedically,

> *"We have no faith in ourselves. I have never met a woman who deep down in her core, really believes she has great legs. And if she suspects she might have great legs, then she's convinced that she has a shrill voice and no neck."*[13]

Ah yes, put in those terms it's easy to see ourselves in that mirror, isn't it?

---

13   Quinn, *Quotations*, page 247.

CHAPTER 6
Civic Engagement

"We pay a price when we deprive children of the exposure to the values, principles, and education they need to make them good citizens."

Justice Sandra Day O'Connor

We hope that this book will prompt mothers/mother figures/mentors to see their potential for shaping our culture in real time through civic and political engagement. The term "civic engagement" leads us to another point. Several courses that have been removed from standard public and even private school curricula need, in our opinion, to be reinstated.

The first course we want to see brought back is Civics. Women and men of a certain age will recall learning the name of their state's senators, their local representatives, the number of senators in the U.S. Senate, and therefore the numbers required for passing legislation and/or overriding vetoes. Liz remembers that years ago when she took her civics course, she learned that Margaret Chase Smith, a U.S. Senator from Maine, was the lone female senator in that body. Liz said she cannot remember the Senator's party, but to this day she remembers her name, and that Ms. Smith had the courage to stand up to Joe McCarthy.

We also learned who the Cabinet members were, how and why they met, and what their roles were. This enabled us to follow the news—in some cases, with as much knowledge and understanding as did our parents. The resulting conversations on politics were a way for many parents and children to share not just information, but life lessons as well. Children learned, for instance, that in some cases their parents opposed new schools not because they opposed better things for their children, but because the required new taxes would put a real hardship on family finances. What a valuable lesson about the way we must learn to judge the pros and cons of various issues! Children thus begin to think in terms of the "big picture," and how an action affects others besides the ones involved in putting it forth.

Your authors thought we had this profound breakthrough in recognizing the lack of a civics education such as we had years ago. We thought it to be somehow at the heart of the lowering of the bar for our elected officials, as well as the rise of incompetency and lack of "big-picture" vision. Yes, we thought we were extremely astute. We are grateful to a knowledgeable friend in education for straightening us out on that before we embarrassed ourselves by patting ourselves on the back in this book and in public!

It turns out that CIRCLE (The Center for Information and Research on Civic Learning and Engagement) at Tufts University's Tisch College has been researching the topic of civics for over ten years. One of their most profound conclusions, is that *civic learning is the best way to train young people to sustain our democracy*. And the *best* way to do it is in and through the schools—presupposing, of course, the existence of good courses, and the presence of good and active teachers.[14] It is easy to see how some of today's teachers have shied away from introducing controversial topics in the classroom because of censure and actual firings that have occurred. That is a shame, because often students listen to teachers to a greater degree than they do their parents. Current events, even when controversial, can be an amazing teaching tool about democracy and how it works. The teachers must, in our opinion, have more support than they

---

14   Jonathon Gould et al., Editor. *Guardian of Democracy: The Civic Mission of Schools.* The Leonore Annenberg Institute for Civics of the Annenberg Public Policy Center at the University of Pennsylvania and the Campaign for the Civic Mission of Schools. https://www.carnegie.org/media/filer_public/ab/dd/abdda62e-6e84-47a4-a043-348d2f2085ae/ccny_grantee_2011_guardian.pdf Accessed June 20, 2018.

currently get in this area. School Boards, and the resident parents in the district owe them their support if they expect the results that turn students into informed voters.

Schools provide two very necessary components for a civics education. The first is that it provides a place where you can associate with others, some of whom will have differing opinions from yours, and differing opinions are critical to avoid groupthink. The second is that attendance at school is mandatory—doubly important for students living where they would not otherwise have that "association" opportunity. Let's discuss this concept of association a bit further.

In a briefing paper called *The Republic is (Still) at Risk—and Civics is Part of the Solution*,[15] prepared for the Democracy at a Crossroads National Summit of September 21, 2017 authors Peter Levine and Kei Kawashima-Ginsberg point out that Americans as a nation no longer "engage in the large connected civic associations that predominated in the twentieth century. Religious congregations and unions were two of the biggest components of civil society…until as recently as 1970." Okay, but what does that have to do with this topic? Oddly enough, quite a bit, they explain.

There is a connection between the group association of people who are non-homogenous and the pursuing of the common goals of our democracy. We think that is incredibly important to remember. By contrast, with the isolation from those who differ in opinion from ourselves, such as we see now, the common goal for our communities and for our country seem to have been lost! Groupthink tends to creep in and take over.

The brief further points out that we see this in particular when those whose distrust for major institutions (religions, banks, corporations, etc.) combines with distrust for other citizens. "The result is declining support for democracy itself."

---

15   Peter Levine, and Kie Kawashima-Ginsberg. *The Republic is (Still) at Risk-and Civics is Part of the Solution.* Medford, MA: Jonathan M. Tisch College of Civic Life, Tufts University, 2017 http://www.civxnow.org/documents/v1/SummitWhitePaper.pdf Accessed June 20, 2018.

Such behavior is infectious. We then start to associate only with people who think as we do, instead of practicing the civics-related skill of keeping an open mind to other points of view and being respectful of another citizen's right to his/her opinion.

It is almost as if debate on an issue—which Maria repeatedly refers to as one of our legislative-process cornerstones—is suddenly unnecessary. You see it every day on Twitter, Facebook, and other social media. We forget to honor not only the process, but also the source of the process (the founding fathers), and their idea that democracy works best when it is in the hands of civically educated and engaged people. It is those civically engaged people who search for and elect candidates meeting criteria for responsible leadership based on our founding principles.

We must never forget, however, that as Col. Jill Morgenthaler, U.S. Army (Ret.) author of the book, *The Courage To Take Command*,[16] often says, "Leaders are not born, they're grown." She reminds us that they do not spring from the womb ready, willing, and capable of leading.

These various statements echo your authors' conclusions—and reinforce the abovementioned paper's assertion that *we need to teach potential leaders things for which they will be held accountable, and most of those things fall under the civics umbrella.* Specifically, the paper calls attention to:

- The art of addressing, considering, and respectfully debating current and controversial issues. That will go a long way to lower the level of both partisanship and personal dislike that currently exists.

- That we all, as Americans living in a democracy (a democratic republic, to be precise) have an obligation to serve. That service need not be in the military. It can—quite appropriately at a student level—be community oriented. Only then can we truly have *a sense* of community.

---

16   Col. Jill Morgenthaler, U.S. Army (Ret.), *The Courage To Take Command,* McGraw-Hill Education, 2015, and discussions with Liz Samuel Richards.

- Students can *have a voice that is heard and that matters*, especially in how they serve. Time and time again in industry we've seen that ownership in one's work results in better output. At this student stage, it builds a foundation for future participation in, and responsibility for, developing and sustaining good government.

- As they engage in service activities and pre- and post-service discussions, students learn to observe and recognize racial and economic disparity, cultivate empathy, and feel an actual eagerness and excitement in digging for the truth of an issue, seeing the value of different perspectives. These are transferable skills, applicable and welcomed in any job, but especially in those that move the economy forward. All these things instill in them the desire to vote, and the habit of doing so, thus sustaining the democracy.

- From both working with and encountering people of different life advantages and views, they understand how diversity of input makes policy decisions better—and we need our leaders to *want* to include diversity as an aspect of all policy decisions. We also want the voters to disapprove of those decisions and policies that don't.

- The media is something that needs to be appreciated and protected. It is our guardian against rampant misdeeds hidden from the public by dishonest, misleading, or corrupt leaders. True journalism has standards—which is why journalists carry (and were given) credentials. Bloggers don't have the same rules, nor do those on social media. They don't have to have sources that will go on record (even if journalists protect those sources.) And they have not (unless it's a newspaper's blog) been hired by respected newspapers or magazines who checked their credentials, their references and their work.

All these things, along with many others, are learned in good civics classes. If we really want to drain the swamp, raise the bar, and all the other clichés that can be applied, it is our opinion that you must start in the early K-12 grades, while at the same time looking at all our roles in the success or failure of our schools. That includes the opportunities (and

civic obligation) to volunteer, or perhaps even run for the school board.
So, if you were wondering how this all tied together, there you go. Run for
the School Board!

This is not a book about civics, but civics obviously plays a vital part. If you want further information on why you should get involved, we are including the names of the references cited here, with their links, in our reference section. If you don't think you're needed, consider this: in 2006 fewer than half of Americans could name the three branches of government. Seriously. It's in the briefing we just cited. Scary. We need to do something, don't we? Start by supporting your local schools. Get involved.

The truth of Justice O'Connor's words about depriving students by not teaching them civics has been obvious over the last ten years. We have seen an erosion of legislative processes, civility, and basic knowledge on the part of many legislators, and legislative candidates. They lack some of the most basic knowledge that could be learned in grade school. We feel civics is both an inherent part of our heritage and our solemn responsibility to embrace as a guide for our own community actions. Maria Montessori, the well-known educator, not only agrees, but expanded the thought, obviously even before and quite independent of Justice O'Connor:

"If education is to be conceived along the same antiquated
lines of a mere transmission of knowledge, there is little to
be hoped from it in the bettering of man's future. For what
is the use of transmitting knowledge if the individual's total
development lags behind." [17]

Maria Montessori

Out of respect for the Justice and her position on civics education, as well as appreciation of her support of civics in general, at least one legislative bill that we know of was named in her honor. Once the *Sandra Day O'Connor Civics Education Act of 2010* passed, that state's legislature approved recurring funding to implement the bill's suggestions.

---

17   Quinn, *Quotations*, page 72.

That avoids the "unfunded mandate" problem educators sometimes face with legislation, where they are given a mandate by the government, and a deadline by which to institute changes within their districts, but are not given any increase in their budget that would allow them to do so.

Here is a perfect example of getting things done that you could implement in your own circumstances in your own community. Ideas don't just belong to one person. Chances are, if you feel passionately about something, someone else does too. All it takes is one or two people to get the ball rolling. Justice O'Connor cared deeply about civics, and traveled across the country, at various times making speeches on the subject. Along the way she found that many other educators and parents shared her sentiments. People began uniting in an effort to see what could be done. Suddenly they were a "force" of the well-known, well-respected, and well-networked.

This is so typical of how things work, both locally and nationally. You need to get the word out about your cause, make yourself a presence in that arena, and you will draw others to you and to your issue. Together these civics advocates figured out what they felt was needed, related it to the institutions involved and persons who carried some weight, and gained traction. It's all about relationships, fueled by passion and respect. It's never, however, a "fast process." But the more you know about the process, the more you know what to expect, and the better equipped you are to deal with it.

Our own state of Illinois moved forward along these lines in 2015. But we know that *all states differ from each other in their undertaking of civics education.* At the time of this writing, Illinois has passed measures requiring high school students to take a semester civics course. Perhaps, helping to publicize these important two studies as we have will be a step toward some level of consistency, even though there will still be state differences based on population, funding, state standards, and many other factors. As with any "movement," once it takes off, counterparts in various states will begin to share experiences in implementing civics legislation at the state level. Again, you will see people who care, lining up with institutions and recognized names. Sometimes stories like this give a birds-eye view of "process" in action that transcend a mere definition.

To that point, we have another story that shows how civics indoctrination *in any form* produces children who grow to adults with a desire to lead, and recognition of the importance of doing so. We spoke with Kathy Ryg and her mother Sheila Schultz, both political veterans. [18]

Sheila began her political career not in politics per se, but as an engaged citizen in a newly developing community. She was asked to pen a column for the local paper, and started following events of the village government. Soon she was supporting a slate of candidates in the local election. Supporting eventually led to running; first winning a seat as Trustee on the Village Board, and later as Village President. During those sixteen years as Village President, she also ran for Cook County Board, a higher office. At that time candidates ran countywide, not by individual district, resulting in lots of territory to cover.

Sheila's oldest daughter, Kathy, had been directly involved in campaigning with her mom for local elections, and joined her again for the county-wide race. Going into racially diverse neighborhoods, markedly different in many ways from her own suburban village, Kathy discovered that they were, in fact, not so different after all. A young mother herself at this point, Kathy saw that the parents' concerns there were the same as in her own town: safe neighborhoods, good schools, reasonable taxes, recreation space for the kids, available jobs for the parents, etc. As a result of this, and many similar experiences learned earlier "at the knee" of her strong mother, Kathy developed a love of civic-minded service and the recognition of a woman's ability to seek and create change.

Before we leave the topic of civics, there is another piece of school curriculum that in a roundabout but important way feeds civics education. And it, too, in most places is currently missing from schools (although we heard a wonderful rumor that it may be coming back to several places throughout the country.) That is the study of cursive writing. It is our opinion that we need to bring back cursive writing. Why? So children are

---

18   Kathy Ryg. Interview with Maria Rodriguez, December 6, 2017, Mundelein, Illinois.

able to read and understand, and hopefully appreciate important historical documents. Documents from centuries prior to the twentieth are most often written rather than typed. It is also an invaluable skill for students at any level to be able to notate documents that either lend credence and validity to their beliefs and theories, or put forth views and beliefs that oppose them. In addition, it enables cursive writers to sign their names more authentically, and send hand-written notes at the many times when still appropriate. That, too, will help them to feel confident about discussing and participating in civics related activities.

CHAPTER 7

A Little Background From Maria

"Only when men are connected to large universal goals are they really happy—and one result of their happiness is a rush of creative activity."

Joyce Carol Oates

Liz is the one who suggested this book and I owe her a great debt. I think it is timely. It also, as I hope you've seen so far, gives me a chance to offer a real perspective on getting involved in politics. While sharing what I learned and what really worked for me, I also hope to save readers from making the same mistakes I did! After all, I have amassed a "war chest" of campaign knowledge I can speak on if politics is the route you choose. We also give you action suggestions throughout the book. Some topics consist of:

- What traits qualify you to run for office, and why

- Questions to ask yourself to determine if you're ready to run

- How the government process works (and why you MUST know this)

- How a campaign should/shouldn't be put together and structured

- Who you need on your campaign staff and what their jobs entail

- How much a local/state/federal campaign can cost, and why it's often an obscene amount

- How to fundraise

- With whom you need to associate, and why
- How to acquire and use data, demographics, and other quantifiable means to target your voters
- Campaign materials – the necessary and the marginal
- TV & Radio and its place in your coverage
- Going door-to-door – which areas to work, and which ask volunteers to handle
- What to say, and when, such as:
  - ☐ Stump speech
  - ☐ Elevator speech
  - ☐ Questions from the Press
  - ☐ Town Hall meetings
- Position papers
- Photo Opps
- Press releases
- Your appearance/image
- When to involve family and how
- Cleaning out your "closet" to remove skeletons
- Opposition research on self & opponent, and at what levels needed
- Why negative campaigning backfires – or does it?
- When to have "no comment"
- Taking care of family:
  - ☐ Preparing them for the campaign
  - ☐ Enlisting their support
  - ☐ Guarding them from mishaps and press ambushes (This generally only happens at the higher office levels.)
- When you misspeak—doing damage control

- Confronting mistakes from your past

- Knowing your own records: both track and voting

- Coming up with needed solutions – and vetting for unintended consequences

- Volunteers:

  ☐ Getting/keeping

  ☐ Training/equipping

  ☐ Dismissing if causing problems

  ☐ Confidentiality/non-disclosure agreements for the staff

- Setting up/maintaining an office

  ☐ The "best" location is a free one

  ☐ How to stock it

- How to debate

- How to address constituent requests for

  ☐ your opinions on an issue

  ☐ your help resolving an issue

- Relations with the media in all its forms – print, electronic, online

- Expenses

  ☐ Defining and allotting funds

  ☐ Controlling & tracking contributions and expenses

- Relations with law enforcement

- Where to show up that will benefit you most

  ☐ Parades

  ☐ Festivals/community celebrations

  ☐ School Board and other civic meetings

- Campaign telephone scripts

  ☐ For you

☐ For volunteers

☐ For office staff in general

☐ Banning robocalls

- Health issues for you and your family, and how to address them:

  ☐ Alcoholism

  ☐ Depression & other mental-health problems

  ☐ Serious physical ailments

- Money issues for you and your family

  ☐ Debt

  ☐ Bankruptcy – personal or business

- Legal issues—why you need an attorney on staff

  ☐ Remember Christine Ferraro (1980's V.P. candidate whose family legal issues caused campaign problems)

  ☐ Suits pending

  ☐ Payment of household help (nannygate)

  ☐ Taxes – any unpaid, any in question

Before we get down to all these "nuts and bolts" items listed above, let's prepare a little by answering many of the *general* questions people always have when considering whether to run. To do that, the end of this chapter will be structured in a Q&A format. As your two authors, we did in fact have this very conversation before agreeing to write this book together—Maria as the experienced candidate who has both run and won and run and lost, and Liz, as the marketing executive and experienced writer eager to document, share, and agree (or argue with) Maria's ideas and experiences. And as Maria says, "Liz represents the typical caring citizen with questions about campaigning and politics whose answers I take for granted because I have been working in politics for many years. She's the female Everyman."

With our collaboration, you'll be getting us as "the real deal." This is who we truly are. And one thing you will come to know about us both is we are anything but terribly formal. Although, this seems like a good time to note that Maria hates dropping in colloquialisms like "just as sure as God made little green apples," or even worse: "aw shucks." So, if you come across one like that, you know Liz snuck it in when Maria wasn't looking!

The other benefit from the Q&A is that you will get a sense of the "spirit" of a candidate as Maria speaks about her experiences running for and holding office, neither sugar coating nor being overly critical with any. That way, you can feel you "know" the person who is giving you the advice, and be comfortable accepting it. So lets take a breath and really get to know Liz and Maria.

So, on with the Q&A. The initial "M" will always refer to Maria, and the initial "L" will always refer to Liz. That will work better than simply "Q" for Question and "A" for Answer, since both of us tend to jump in as we think of something.

M. Before we get started, Liz, I want to thank you for suggesting this book. Your questions have ensured that many of the details are here that might otherwise have been overlooked.

L. You're very welcome! I think I was a bit like your barometer for whether someone who had never run for office understood what you were saying. You know, the canary in the coal mine kind of thing.

M. Yep.

L. OK, Maria, let's talk about *you* for a moment so the readers get to know you better and maybe even see themselves in you. First of all, as a child, when someone asked you what you wanted to be, did you ever see yourself as a political person?

M. No! I was very shy growing up; politics was not even a remote possibility. I did make a concerted effort to push myself past the shyness, and eventually became more sure of myself. My husband and I had three children in four years, and I quickly discovered that signing your kids up for some sport or activity often included volunteering. Many women are familiar with the fact that first you agree to be the "math mom" or "room mother." And once your face is "out there," you're soon working the concession stand or helping to coach a park district team, etc. As time goes on, you end up *running* the concession stand or chaperoning at band camp, or heading up the fundraiser for the church. My point is, like many women, that is what led me to politics. In the same spirit of volunteerism, I said, "Sure, I can help out as the Village Clerk." This goes to the reason we are writing this book. Women typically need to be talked into running for political office, yet we have often been doing the same tasks in many other organizations.

L. Oh! I read about that—about women having to be talked into it. The surprising reason why they need to be talked into it? According to

Susannah Wellford, co-founder of *Running Start*, it's because we don't feel capable![19] She points out that 80% of men will apply for a job if they don't meet all the skill or experience requirements, because they assume they will *grow into it*. On the other hand, 80% of women will only apply if they meet each and every asked-for skill or suggested amount of experience. This same statistic also appears in several books on women and leadership. Amazing, yes?

M. Yes, although I didn't know the statistics, I know that it is unfortunately true. I hope we soon develop the confidence to be a bit more like the men in that respect. Anyway, back to your question. I did not grow up in a family that was politically active. However, in retrospect, I was probably influenced by my Aunt Jane being mayor of her small town in Oklahoma when I was in high school. It is ironic that you called me about this book idea on the very day she died, Liz. Your idea for a book called *Run Jane, Run...We Need You In Office!* definitely struck a chord. I love the nod toward the vintage early reading primers, *Fun With Dick and Jane*, since this is a "primer" on getting involved in politics. And the irony was just too good to pass up, since my Aunt Jane was the first "real person" I ever knew who ran for political office.

L. Cool.

M. You know, my Aunt Jane was really remarkable. While working as Mayor, she was also raising nine children and helping her husband, who was a rural doctor/surgeon, run a medical clinic. All this, while he was simultaneously on staff at three local rural hospitals. I bring that up because it illustrates an important point about the way women think. Remember I said they think differently, with different parts of their brains than men do?

L. Yes.

M. Well, as I said, Aunt Jane's family had grown to nine children, and their current house was no longer big enough. But, when Uncle George

---

19   Claire Landsbaum. *How to Get More Women Involved in Politics.* The Cut: New York Magazine, November 16, 2016. https://www.thecut.com/2016/11/how-to-get-more-women-involved-in-politics.html Accessed June 20, 2018.

was offered a job as a rural doctor and surgeon, they jumped at it because to compensate for the rural location and still lure a fine doctor, the package included use of the large U-shaped building that was the clinic. The way the building was laid out, Aunt Jane instinctively knew they could use one wing as a clinic, and the remaining wing as a home with bedrooms for all the children as well as themselves. It worked, and Aunt Jane raised her family while being an integral part of the community. Big picture thinking; multiple problems solved.

L. Yowie, nine kids! I don't know how she did it. I'm sure she'd be pleased about the title of the book and the fact that you are remembering her with such admiration.

M. Oh, I know she would. But she's the kind of woman who would simply say quite humbly that she was glad to have helped me along. That's another thing my aunt typified: the humble grace of strong women.

Actually, I was greatly influenced *by all of the women* in my mother's family, each one a story in herself. But that is not uncommon. In fact, it is typically the rule rather than the exception with strong women: we influence each other by simply existing and doing what our moral compass tells us to. We don't *set out* to be an influence. It's just the natural order of things. In fact, Liz, you should tell the story about the waitress in California.

L. Yes, I probably should, but later; I want to stay on track with you right now. But I will say this: that's how I became so active in *my* community—being around my dear friend, Andrea, who was always getting involved and going where her moral compass led her. We talk a lot, you and I, about the moral compass, don't we?

M. Yes, we do, because I think it's often missing today in a whole lot of people.

L. Agreed. Now, where were we? Oh yes, how you were influenced by your mother's female relatives. Give me a couple examples, why don't you? What were the kinds of things, the kinds of traits or skills or habits that were passed down from one to the other?

M. Well, to start with, they were *each* the embodiment of what I consider to be a strong woman, so it was all around me. My little grandmother—and I mean *literally* little at around five feet—raised seven children. Each of her daughters had large families, was well educated, and was influential in the lives of all forty-five cousins. You don't see big families like that too much anymore, do you?

L. Not too much.

M. Well, it seemed pretty much normal to us at the time. Though we are scattered all over the world, today many of us continue to remain close. Anyway, these strong woman have influenced me and all my cousins all through our lives by simply "taking care of business."

L. You don't mean they worked outside the home, though, right?

M. Actually, yes, they worked outside the home, and most of them went back to school to get a Master's Degree while raising these large families. Truly amazing women. With a family that big, you experience all life has to offer. They showed us how to work together to overcome challenges and accomplish incredible things.

They also showed us how to live when the unthinkable happens. With forty-five grandchildren, you were bound to see your share of tragedies. Some worse than others, of course, and some that seemed almost beyond a person's ability to bear. But these women bore them, with a deep faith, a sense of self confidence that they could heal heartache for their loved ones, and a perseverance to suggest true inner strength. I certainly didn't fully appreciate their example until I had children of my own.

(Smiles) And you know what? They always saw the humor in things. Always! My memory of them when they were together was of howling laughter. So, I grew up thinking *that's what a strong woman looks like*. She looks like me, and my mother, and her sisters. I don't think there was ever a time when something was so wrong that they couldn't eventually make it right, or so hurtful that it couldn't be smoothed over. The legacy continues in my cousins, who learned by osmosis the benefits of deep soulful conversations peppered with side-splitting laughter.

L. So, this is where you got the first sense that these basic leadership skills must be innate characteristics of strong women—if they choose to use them?

M. That's right. You must *choose* to use them. You see examples of this all the time. The breakup of a marriage, the loss of a child, the death of a parent will absolutely decimate some women, while others go on to survive and succeed, even thrive! And even others go on to forge a movement that builds on the loss or the sacrifices, like Candy Lightner did with MADD (Mothers Against Drunk Drivers) in 1980 after her fifteen-year old daughter was killed by one.

I have to wonder if some women are just not aware of these potential leadership traits lying dormant inside them. In speaking to women specifically about these innate qualities, I am more confident than ever that mothers and mentors are instinctive leaders. The qualities they possess to "mother" can be used effectively in so many other ways and in so many other areas! And while it's true of mothers, it's also true that there are many single women who use and hone those same skills in a wide variety of ways every day.

L. How so?

M. Well, think about it. Usually at work, situations arise where someone has to step up and be the leader. They need to calm an explosively charged situation, recognize all voices, weigh all options and make a considered judgment. On top of that, they also mentor interns, break in new programs, and make sure everyone understands them, just as a mother helps a child learn new skills—though in this case, the learning techniques are much more advanced.

In many cases, these single women who fill our workforce at various levels also take children under their wings through Big Brothers/Big Sisters, YMCA/YWCA, Church, youth and/or sports groups, or even by simply being the favorite aunt who kids love having for a visit. There are so many ways to nurture…as many as there are women.

And let's take a minute for a sidebar here. As the number of successful women has increased, among them there has been a return to a more natural and inclusive mentoring process. Several decades ago that was not always the case, and I'm glad to see women embracing mentoring more fully again. We are not each other's enemy; we are each other's support. We need not diminish anyone to advance ourselves.

It should be a constant wave of motion up and down—all of womanhood in motion to support and mentor each other. As you and I have said many times, every woman who "makes it" up the ladder should turn around and extend a hand to the one coming up behind her. It would make such a difference in all our lives if women formed one big wave, those at the top reaching down to help those in the middle who are likewise at the same time reaching those just coming up at the entry level below them. If you look at it from the bottom up and assign "labels" to groups, you could have the Millennials coming in at the entry, but mentoring upward, teaching the Gen-Xers all the newest things in technology, and then Gen-Xers pass that on up to Boomers, while at the same time, those Boomers are passing lore and success tips down to the Gen-Xers, who in turn are mentoring the Millennials, giving them mid-management skills that only come from experience.

We just spoke in business terms for management and mentoring, but of course the same thing used to be true in motherhood when multi generations lived near to each other, unlike many cases today, where families are far-flung. Grandmothers mentored mothers, who were teaching their own children, who in turn kept them current on the latest things in education, trends, etc. Now friends and neighbors who are also mothers sometimes fill those roles. The point is, mentoring is alive and well. **The more you observe human interaction anywhere at all, you start to see the inter-relation of these mentoring/ mothering skills and how they transfer to leadership positions.**

L. So, you're saying married, unmarried, mother or not, all women have mothering and mentoring skills; they simply apply them differently, and those skills transfer to basic leadership skills, and political ones as well?

M. Absolutely! I know one woman who devoted her life to politics in a wide variety of offices and appointments. Her name is Penny Pullen, and although she never had children of her own, she influenced many. I was telling her about my research for this book on that very topic, when she shared a story with me. During her tenure as Illinois State Representative, she had a male intern named Jeremy who considered her a true mentor. Years after they had worked together, he called to let her know that he, now a Navy Intelligence Officer, and his wife were going to name their new daughter after her! Just think about it, the influence women exert that they aren't even aware of until someone points it out.

L. You keep telling me to think about things a lot.

M. Sorry about that—well, wait a minute, no I'm not! We just don't think about these things enough when we evaluate our skillsets. Women are often as well educated as men. They have the desire to better their community in one way or another; they relate to being able to control chaos—have you ever been to a six-year old's birthday party?? And rather than send their sons off to war, they would rather negotiate a peace. Plus, they are experts at making rules that make most everyone happy at once. If that's not what a good politician does, I don't know what is.

L. Agreed. So, let's get to actually *showing* women how to utilize these skills in more ways than they ever probably thought about, then show them how to get elected, and give them a list of additional organizations, books, and other resources that can also help them. First, though, just so readers feel comfortable that you know whereof you speak, let's hear a little bit about how you got started in politics. You know, what was the deciding factor that made you take the leap?

M. Well, this book is being written to give a real face to volunteering, then building on that experience to work in politics, campaigning either for someone you believe in, or eventually for yourself. It's also meant to show women everywhere that when they look at themselves through a leadership lens they will be shocked, I'm sure, at the huge number of leadership skills they already possess. I know I was. And as said in the first pages of the book, it's exactly the leadership our country sorely needs. No matter the party, no matter the sex, we must have leaders who once again elevate our culture from the lower level of ethics we have come not only to accept, but to expect. We shape the country the way we want it to be, Liz. So, let me tell you my political story, and perhaps the readers will see themselves a bit; and perhaps they too will be inspired to run.

L. Go for it.

M. My political life began to take shape in my early forties.

L. Did you say "forties?"

M. Absolutely. A huge number of women are starting new careers and ventures in their forties, fifties—and even older. In this day and age, if economically feasible, there are enough options that a woman can either raise a family first and then start a career in her forties or later; choose to remain single and start a career right away in her twenties; or have a career early on and then take time from it to raise a family, going back to her career later. For example, didn't you tell me you took a job in California and drove cross country by yourself to get there when you were fifty, and opened your own agency when you were sixty?

L. Indeed I did! And I'm so glad I did both. I chose the option (although it was almost de rigueur back then) of raising my family first and then going back to work. Which was kind of cool, because more job areas had opened for women by that time than there had been twenty years earlier. But yes, I drove from Chicago to Palm Springs, then Los Angeles all by myself over three days for that job. What a hoot!

M. I thought so. It seems we each had a moment in time where we suddenly saw ourselves as we wanted to be, or knew at least that we wanted to be different than we were at that point. More well-rounded, perhaps, more advanced in our goals, or simply different in some undefined way. You, in sales at the time, wanted to be in an environment where you were respected as a professional and successful salesperson, not as the "rookie" that everyone at your current company still saw you as. You knew somewhere in your gut that you were so much more than a rookie, knew so much more than you did previously, and wanted to be a part of making things happen at the highest levels.

And I, a busy volunteering homemaker at the time, saw myself in politics, but not quite at the very beginning. I did know, however, that there were more, and different, things I wanted to accomplish. The point is we each had our "awakening," a moment in time when we either said "Enough!" or when we said, "I want to do more."

At the time, of my own awakening, I was the mother of three, working part time as the Liturgy Coordinator at our church. Since I had been quite shy as a girl, it took a determined effort to get me out of my comfort zone. So, it stands to reason, I wasn't a very accomplished speaker in my early days (smiles). But I found volunteering to be a great stepping stone, and motherhood had already included enough parent-volunteer projects to fill three resumes. So that grew my confidence more and more with each venture. And then I had my "pivotal moment," as I call it. Perhaps readers have already had theirs, just like we had ours. Perhaps that's why they're reading this book. But mine came (where else?) at the dinner table.

I was at a dinner party and I heard someone say they were fifty-two years old, and just realized they wouldn't be doing all the things they thought they would in life. Wow. That stopped me, fork in mid-air. That was too true and hit so close to home that I felt it was no coincidence for me to hear it. It dawned with a thud that I had become totally complacent—so involved with the ongoing everyday minutia, that I hadn't been seeing how months were turning into years. And if I didn't wake up, suddenly I too might be too old or not healthy enough to do all the things I wanted.

That thought really shook me up, and the next day I decided to change things. I wanted to be able to say, "I will" and "I did" a whole lot more than "I guess I won't" or "I wish I had." So, I started with one thing. I started running—physically running, not running for office!

To be clear, I was not somebody who was either in prime physical condition or who considered herself to be *at all* athletic. But the odd thing is, I got good at it. Good enough that I couldn't help but wonder what *else* had I not done that I might indeed be good at? They say timing is everything, and boy did I see that first hand! There's a quote by Diane Ackerman, author of *The Zookeeper's Wife*, that says "I don't want to get to the end of my life and find that I just lived the length of it. I want to have lived the width of it as well." That pretty much sums up what I was feeling.

As fate would have it, just as I was mulling over that question, someone suggested I run for an office. The irony was not lost on me. I hadn't ever thought I would be a good athletic runner, and I was now *more* than good. Now I was being asked to stretch myself once again. My children were in high school and college, and so my time commitments had changed. Talk about your life-changing moments!

We'll be sharing what I learned to do, and what not to do, while running a campaign. By the way, I guess I was considered the longshot during my first campaign because I ran against a well-known and successful business executive. He was thought to outrank me in every category. Ah, but he had never been a mother, or a mothering figure! I truly think that made the difference. Not only did I have the passion and the deep desire to win, I had the leadership traits that I had perfected (okay, maybe not perfected, but certainly honed) as a mother, and as a volunteer. And I could relate to the everyday concerns of the people in my town. As time went on, I felt truly equipped.

What I learned from that—and this is important to our theories here— is that your future goals will not, *nor should they ever,* line up exactly with your past or present responsibilities. But that shouldn't limit you. All the skills you acquire along the way *are* transferable.

Many of us, especially women, have abilities, potential, and strengths that are hidden under the ordinary routine of our lives. Don't let that remain the case! Seriously, don't let it. Even if you're scared (and sometimes terrified), push yourself to keep trying new things. You will find that pushing through fear, learning, and practicing, will lead you farther than you ever dreamed of going. I know that sounds like some platitude spouted to sound inspirational, but it is true beyond belief. Especially in politics.

L. You sound so passionate about that!

M. I really am.

L. OK, let's say everyone gets the maximum possible out of this book. What would you hope that would be?

M. Well, I have to answer that in two parts. First, I want the women who feel "less than equipped" when they compare themselves to others to feel confident that they already possess the needed skills for the job.

L. The innate ones we've discussed?

M. Yes, of course those, but many women have also acquired additional ones that further support those. So, second, I want them to know that those same skills can be influential in either mothering or changing the world—often doing both, and being a role model for both children and adults as they do. Isn't that amazing that you could change the world?

L. Indeed.

M. And I think changing the world starts with civic engagement and leads in one way or another to political involvement, even if not running for office. But here's the thing; if they *do* choose to run, I want them to not only be comfortable with the idea of running for office, but also to know what to expect overall, and what to look out for. Not only the nuts and bolts of a campaign, like who they need to hire to run it, how to check backgrounds and what to expect daily, but also the emotional tolls and rewards of political office.

L. Sounds like a lot to take in.

M. I know it sounds that way, but don't forget, women are good at seeing the big picture and how it all fits together.

L. I thought men were good at that?

M. I'm really glad you said that, because women have been underestimated for years on this "big-picture" skill. Hopefully we can help change that.

L. OK, let's address a couple of the things you just mentioned. How do you deal with the emotions that must be so prevalent in the campaign, whether you win or lose?

M. Well, yes, there are emotions, certainly, and sometimes it's like a roller coaster. That's why it's so important to have someone you can trust to *never* be a "yes man." This is true both while campaigning and while in office. You need objectivity around you to keep you on track and focused. Over-confidence could, sadly, keep you from visiting critical places that are rich with votes, thinking you already have them in the bag. By the same token, while in office it is equally important to stay focused in the midst of a plethora of opinions trying to sway yours.

For me, it was my husband, Ray, who kept me grounded. I always knew I could count on him to say, "Shake it off" or "Maybe the guy's right." While I was Mayor, he was my sounding board from the start. Initially, I took office after a contentious election in our small town, and it was a little rocky, to say the least. There were six Village Trustees, three of whom had strongly supported my opponent. I remember one morning telling Ray about the previous night's meeting and the frustration turned to tears as I spoke. I wasn't sad, though; I was frustrated.

His response was not a comforting hug...he looked at me with his face sort of scrunched up and said, channeling Tom Hanks from the movie, *A League of Their Own,* "Wait, are you crying? There's no CRYING in politics...there's NO crying in politics." And then he said something that shifted my perspective and got me back on track. He said, "You need to actually BE the mayor. I know that you are

completely capable, but you need to SEE YOURSELF THAT WAY."
It was hard to hear, but he was right. I stopped worrying about what
if I screwed something up, and focused on what needed to be done.
In time, the board worked well together, and we accomplished a great
deal, even though we were plagued by a recession midway through
the second term. As you can see, it *always, always* comes back to
self-perception.

And you do need a thick skin. Campaigns can be brutal, and they
always have been. But with the advances and prevalence of social
media, they seem to be even more so today. I can tell you firsthand
that developing a thick skin is an incredible bonus to your entire life.
It changes you in so many ways...you end up standing comfortably in
your own skin, knowing exactly what you're made of.

Part of developing thick skin consists of addressing disparaging or
threatening issues immediately and diffusing them in a fairly low-key
way. Your thick skin helps you rise above the tendency to "fight back"
and look like you're throwing a tantrum, or worse, denying something
that's obviously concerning.

L. Speaking of brutal, what does that do to your family?

M. Ah, yes, your family. Well, they should have been in on your decision
process from the very beginning, especially if you run for a high-profile office. They have to understand that some people won't agree with
you, and some people will say awful things about you, but that's all
part of "it." The first thing you must recognize is that it's up to *YOU* as
the candidate to protect your family; and one of the ways you do that
is by preparing them.

L. And how do you do that?

M. By making them aware that these negative things are to be expected,
and not to be surprised by them. Unless you are running for one of
those very high-profile offices we mentioned, they leave your kids
alone...unless they get picked up by the police. If they get picked
up by the police, even if they didn't do anything wrong I would be

lying if I said that it wasn't a problem. Knowing that, they need to be especially aware of what they are doing, always thinking about their choices and the consequences that come with them.

L. Oh my God! Did your kids get picked up by the police?

M. No (laughing) but it has happened to others, and I've seen it. So have you, if you think about it.

L. Our most recent presidents have all had young children while serving in the White House. The Clintons, Bushes and the Obamas all come to mind in that respect, and can be credited with doing what it took to make their girls feel comfortable.

M. Exactly. And I'm sure it wasn't as simple as it looked!

L. What else?

M. You also try to think of any skeletons in the closet that might come out at some point. Sometimes it's something dumb you did as a teenager and haven't thought about for years. Or it may be something more serious that a relative did. If it should come up, that's when family members need to say, "You'll have to ask the candidate if she wishes to discuss that." They can be pleasantly firm, without being rude. Rude is not usually a good choice.

I think most people can handle what they *know* might be coming at them. It's the unknown or the unexpected that usually throws people. There's not a family in this country that doesn't have some issue or some relative they'd rather not discuss. They don't disown them; they just keep them out of the limelight as much as possible.

L. Let's tackle another topic about campaigning. Is there much difference in running for city council or for mayor than there is for state or national office?

M. Well, a small town where you are campaigning, or in office already, knows pretty much everything about you—and your family! If they have a question or if there's a problem you need to address, the townspeople there simply stop you when they see you. That's even true, to a certain extent, when you run for state senator or state representative, because you're running from your own district, which is a bit of a de-facto small town. So, it's not all that dissimilar. But running for governor, lieutenant governor, U.S. senator or any other state or national office is a whole different ball game.

L. How so? Can you be more specific?

M. Well, as you move up to running for the higher elected offices, you have to *show* people who you are and what you stand for. Most of them don't already know.

Also, especially in some of the larger states, there are pockets of differences within the state itself. For instance, here in Illinois, the northern part of the state contains Chicago, making it and the surrounding suburbs more cosmopolitan, for better or worse, than the central or southern parts of the state, which has traditionally been farmland and more rural in atmosphere. And some places in southern Illinois actually border on the Mason-Dixon Line.

And it's not merely a difference between city or suburban life and farm life. It can be a cultural difference as well. This is typical for geographically large states. Northern California, for instance, is culturally different that Southern California, and each takes pride in those differences. As a result, in every large state—or in any state for that matter—you must be aware of those differences, and the challenges they present.

Once you're aware of these differences, you see them yourself. Some areas will be more concerned about jobs than they will be about maintaining open lands. Some will be looking to do something about being in a food desert, while other areas will have an abundance of food choices through farm stands, co-ops, and multiple grocery stores. Roads will concern some, crime others; and it will be your job as the candidate to know which areas care about which issues, and to care about them also. Candidates who do not connect with the people— or have their ear to the ground—will not get the votes they need to be elected.

L. Wow. Sounds daunting.

M. It can be, but that's where an experienced campaign staff can be invaluable. As a matter of fact, here's a good quote for you, and it probably applies to your campaign manager more than anyone else. It's from Oprah, and you know Oprah, she says things pretty clearly. She says, "Lots of people want to ride with you in the limo, but what you want is someone who will take the bus with you when the limo breaks down." So, what I'm saying is a lot of these issues will be covered by an alert campaign manager: making sure you know where you are and whom you're addressing. So make sure it's someone you can trust, who really wants you to succeed and isn't just along for the limo ride. We'll give some more info on spotting the right characteristics later when we talk about staffing.

L. I heard Jack Kennedy had a great system for giving the right speech to the right people that kept the speechwriting to a minimum, but laser focused.

M. Indeed he did. How did you know about that?

L. I read a lot.

M. You brought it up, want to run with it?

L. Sure, I heard that he kept every speech to three sections, and two were always basically the same. The first was always about the Democratic party and its goals for the country, since he was a Democrat. He told how he espoused them, citing how they would help the nation.

M. That's right. Since I was running as a Republican, my remarks were rooted in Republican themes.

L. That's OK, I like you anyway!

M. Very funny. Actually, though, that's an important point, isn't it?

L. You bet. People should be able to disagree about an issue, but recognize it as simply that, an issue, and deal with that, not with each other's personalities.

OK, back to Kennedy. So, after he would first talk about the party per se, he would have a second part that talked about the things *that specific audience* would care about. Then the third part was a wrap up of how he saw things going forward, and was roughly equivalent to what was used for a "stump speech." So sections one and three could always remain approximately the same wherever he went and whomever he addressed. The second or central portion is the one that would change every time. How fitting that it was the central section that changed, because those were the issues that were "central" to that audience. Something to emulate, I'd say.

M. Believe me, many people do, including myself. I think it's one of the keys to successful speaking. To imagine electing you, people need to clearly see you as a surrogate for their own voices; they need to know you can fully articulate and empathize with their issues.

We hope that putting public speaking in such simple terms will help you to see yourself as a candidate, because you can't be anybody's voice at the table if you don't run. As the famous hockey player Wayne Gretzky said, and I paraphrase here "You *may* miss 50% of the shots you take, but you will *definitely* miss 100% of the ones you don't."

L. I like that. As a matter of fact, it's one of my mantras for stepping up.

M. I'm not surprised!

L. Other than the things you just mentioned about your having to run to win, what else is different as you tackle a run for a higher office?

M. Well, we get into it more in later chapters of the book, but it's about layers. In the small-town races (Library Board, Park District, City Clerk, etc.) you really don't need to have volunteers in such massive numbers. And you also don't need a full paid staff for a local run. Sometimes, however, you may have the same-titled staff, but give him/her assistants in the larger races. It's numbers, layering, press outreach, and of course costs that escalate as you climb the ladder of offices.

L. OK, moving right along, and sticking with the emotional side of a campaign, do you have to change the way you view things, and perhaps even the way you think?

M. Well, yes and no.

L. You sound like a true politician.

M. (Laughs) Well, I guess I am, but I wince just a bit at that title because of the negative connotations currently attached to it. That's another thing I hope this book does—change the way some disillusioned skeptics look at politicians.

But back to your question about changing your view. The one thing you *NEVER* should change are your core values. They make you who you are and act as your moral compass, guiding you in the issues where you must take a stand. And those stands are important. Your position on an issue can *evolve* over time if the issue is a complicated one and you learn more details. But you've seen, I'm sure, how unattractive and destructive to a campaign it is to be seen as flip-flopping. Evolving yes, flip-flopping, no. Any intelligent, thinking person will pay attention to the issues and as he or she learns more, will be able to better see both sides. I wouldn't say that is changing your view; *I would say that is expanding your view, which is a good thing, not a bad one.*

The other side of that, of course, is that there are two sides to an issue. When you choose what you feel is the best solution, only one side will be happy. But at least your constituents will know where you stand, which is really very important. Hopefully it will be where most of them stand too! Equally important, I would say is to make sure they know WHY you stand for what you do. It makes it easier for them to respect your position if they understand it, and can agree to disagree.

One other thing that happens as you do this is that you find yourself taking on a *persuasive mindset.* Your family will probably notice it even before you do. It kind of just happens. All the time. You are ready to persuade anyone about anything that comes up.

L. When a campaign is over, do you find that you look at your friends differently?

M. I think there is more to that question than what you are asking me. Are you asking if your friends drop you, or if you drop them?

L. Yeah, I guess I was.

M. No to both. If you are really good friends they have been on board the campaign from the get go, and when you are talking about the issues you are actually telling them what you've learned. You become grateful for the support of the friends who love politics and even more grateful to those who hate politics, but were in it because they love you. But to tell you the truth, the conversation with your really close friends aren't as issue oriented as they are campaign-progress related.

And, on the plus side, if you find that you passionately agree on a particular issue, and take similar stands, it can bring you closer. That's another reason I say it's like being on a roller coaster—you never know what will come up next, or what you'll discover that either totally surprises you or confirms what you already believed. It's an education, to say the least. And a big bonus is that you'll wind up meeting a lot of people, some of whom will become great friends.

L. So, who do you "hang out" with during a campaign? Old friends, new friends, or both?

M. Well, perhaps this is going to sound harsh but the truth of the matter is that time and money are limited during a campaign, and you have one goal: getting elected. So it's really critical to keep your eye on that goal and make the most of the time you do have. That entails spending time and working with the people that can help you achieve your goal. And that breaks down to the people who can vote for you, get their friends to vote for you, and contribute to your campaign war chest by either donating money themselves or by hosting fund raisers.

L. That's kind of self-serving, isn't it?

M. Yeah, I guess it really is, especially during a campaign for higher office. The final months feel like a mad race to the finish. You're packing a minute and a half into every minute, and still knowing that you may be missing some one thing or person that would be central to your winning.

L. Okay, you mentioned getting the most mileage, given time constraints by spending that time with certain people and organizations. I get that. And I get the idea that your time even when socializing is campaign oriented. Which brings me back to my question about how do you begin to find the audiences that you're looking for? Let's expand a bit on who those people would be.

M. Well, let's start with who they *wouldn't* be. You may think that you put on the back burner family and friends and people whose vote you feel sure of, but the opposite is actually the case. They, in fact, are the "inner circle" who attend a lot of events with you to serve several purposes. In addition to introducing you as someone they know and trust, they also help people to meet the candidate one-on-one and build your base of followers.

L. You're saying you spend time with people who want to help get votes.

M. Yes, as many additional votes as possible. And that means:

- asking your already committed friends to talk you up to all *their* friends.

- going to as many multi-person exposures as you can. Speak *anywhere* they'll have you!

- meeting people at train stations early in the morning and after work. Say hello, give them a brochure (more on brochures later) and ask them to call your office with any concerns they want you to care about on their behalf. Let them see you, hear your voice, and get the sense that you care. That's one of the most valuable ways to use your time—meeting them on their level and where they are.

L Wouldn't that mean you'd have to have a bazillion different speeches ready at once?

M. Aha! That's why people need this book: I talk about that in the chapters on how to conduct the actual campaign. One of the things that

I suggest when you're not doing a special occasion speech (during which you can copy Kennedy's three-section method) is to rely on your stump speech, knowing it backward and forward, even sideways and out of order till you can say it in your sleep. Which at some point, you probably actually will do! Your stump speech is your best friend during any campaign appearance.

L. What do you mean, your best friend?

M. Well it does everything but hold your coat while you talk. Seriously, it serves multiple purposes. Here's how: you come up with a ten-minute speech—just ten minutes—that covers the three basic platforms on which you're running.

L. I notice you're using the number three again.

M. I know. For some reason it seems to work.

L. Woody Allen used it in his comedy writing too, you know.

M. No, I didn't.

L. Well that's another story, but things in threes seem to pack a punch. For instance, interior designers always suggest displaying your decorative pieces in groups of three as well. Must be a thing.

M. Where do you come up with this stuff?

L. I told you, I read a lot. And I'm a very eclectic reader. Before the Obama/Romney election, for instance I read eight political books—some from the left and some from the right.

M. (Rolls eyes) Well, back to the stump speech. Once you've selected your three basic platforms and written them clearly and concisely, you memorize them as I said, frontward, backwards, and sideways until you can say them in your sleep.

L. OK, but I don't understand "sideways."

M. I use sideways to mean you can pull a sentence or two out from anywhere in the speech to use as an answer to a question. That comes in especially handy with the press, and has the added benefit of reinforcing that you believe in your program enough to repeat and emphasize it. Don't be afraid to repeat the exact same sentence over and over again. That both helps you stay on message and prevents you from using the wrong words. It also helps keep reporters at bay.

You can also pull parts out to answer questions from people who stop you on the street, or to address things that come up in even casual conversations at fundraisers. It is your "wingman" so to speak. Again, don't vary the words, and don't "expound" on it, trying to be conversational. Don't forget, your stump speech is your wingman, and you have a wingman for *one* purpose—to keep you apprised of what you need to know as he/she guides you and helps you keep your eye on your target. And your target is satisfying with consistent, clear, and concise answers the person who can get you elected.

L. One thing I wanted to follow up on is earlier you said that it's vital for a potential candidate to understand the political process. Can you speak to that a bit more? I'm still a bit confused to how the process of passing a law is similar to the process of getting elected.

M. I'm not sure I understand what you're saying. When I refer to the process I'm referring to the American governmental process, which is the necessary debate over an issue at various levels that finally leads to a vote for sustainable legislation. I don't think that campaigning is a process as much as it is a series of milestones with a variety of ways to get there. The governernmental process is dictated by the Constitution. Although there are various milestones in a campaign to be met, they are met in different ways for different offices and by different candidates.

It's one thing to know what you want to accomplish by passing and enacting laws. That's great, and it's a good start; but without understanding the process and traditions and procedural requirements for getting those laws passed, you just wont't have laws that can stand the test of time.

L. What? English, please.

M. That's why you have debates, hearings, all of that. If there are conflicts between different entities the law would serve, they usually surface during those debates, and the proposed law can then take those conflicts into consideration. In doing that, the law can be adapted, rather than have the conflicts pointed out later and have the law overturned as a result.

L. Okay, I see the difference, but to a non-political person like me a process always meant the series of ordained steps to accomplish something, and that something could be anything.

M. It's not always foolproof, but it's as close humanly possible. Every once in a while an exception proves the rule.

L. Oh, and I know of an example of when that happened. It's an old example from the late 1980's or 1990's, but it's a good one, I think. In our desire to clean up both our internal and external environments, we could, without the full hearings, debates, etc. have a conflict like we did with the issue of dangerous fumes from the factory floor during the manufacturing and assembly of electronic circuit boards. OSHA comes into the facility and says that for the safety of the workers on the floor, and even in the adjacent offices, they can't have the fumes from the chemicals—the soldering, the flux and the cleaning solutions—running rampant at that time as VOC's (volatile organic compounds). They have to be extracted from the production floor. So, the facility says okay, we'll vent them up through ducts to the outside air where they will dissipate. I bet you can see where this is going, Maria.

M. I bet I can too.

L. So, they vent them to the outside and next thing you know, the EPA (Environmental Protection Agency) comes along and says sorry, Mr. Facility Manager, you can't vent that to the outside. You're polluting our air. So here you are…two well-meaning laws, enacted but conflicting. There are more recent examples but I won't cite them because I don't want to sound partisan, since that was one thing we swore not to do in this book. (Thinking a minute) Wow. There really is a lot to learn, isn't there?

M. Sure, but not so much that it should be a deterrent to running. It's easy to pick up, and that's why we're writing this book! I want women to know it's not rocket science. Once you learn the rules—and the pit-falls—then then you can play the game. Then it's as easy as any other challenging but fulfilling task they have already undertaken. And the governmental process is SLOW by design for the reasons we just mentioned. Believe me, I know that to be true..

L. Okay, so let's talk a little more about campaigning. I can imagine what it feels like to win. What should someone expect to feel, if they lost a race that meant a lot to them?

M. First of all, you have to acknowledge it really is an emotional blow. It doesn't lay you so low, however, that you can't carry on. I don't think anyone encapsulates losing with grace despite the inner pain and disappointment better than John McCain. I saw him at a fundraiser after he had lost the presidential election, and when asked how he was doing after his dramatic loss to Barack Obama he calmly said "Oh I sleep like a baby…sleep a few hours then get up and cry. Sleep for two more hours then wake up and cry some more." That is paraphrased a bit, but it's pretty close. It turned out to be such an effective line that he later repeated it on late night television. Nothing heals better than a sense of humor in the face of what's really not all that funny because it hurts!

L. So, I guess the best thing to do is to win! Then you obviously don't have to deal with losing!

M. Right! But you also have to remember that you can always run again, and there is no dishonor in losing—disappointment, yes; dishonor, no. The political arena is one area where you are respected for having run—even if you didn't win.

L. One more thing, though. There are probably a lot of women out there who, for a variety of reasons, don't necessarily want to run, but want very much to help those women who *have* decided to. Should they read this book too?

M. Absolutely! There is nothing more valuable to a candidate than a knowledgeable volunteer. This book will give the volunteers an understanding of the journey required to get someone elected. They can then more easily see how they could fit in and help the candidate of their choice.

And by the way, I know many women like that—women who have decided they are not the one to be the candidate, but they still have a burning desire to make a difference. They most often have excellent supplies of grit and determination; and grit and determination win the day.

It begins by having determination to *do* what's best, and *get* what's best for their children, other family members, or even themselves. They do it through schooling, through jobs, and basically through opportunities in every area of their lives. Acting on those goals with a focus and force that's pretty much unbeatable—even if they do it from behind the scenes or within the parameters of someone else's campaign, it's the "desired results that they are fighting for and hope to achieve."

They make excellent volunteers. As a matter of fact, we talk later in the book a great deal about volunteers, and the roles they can play. Nowhere was that more apparent than in the Bernie Sanders 2016 campaign. But as I said, more on that later.

L. Super. That should encourage **all** our readers, not just the candidates themselves, that they have a voice that needs to be heard and shared. I hope they do get involved in some capacity.

M. Me too! They are so valuable and, unfortunately, many times don't realize it. Maybe this book will change that!

L. I hope so.

L. Well, Maria, you have quite a story so far, and I must say, very relatable. So, moving into the "nuts and bolts" that you promised, let's end this Q&A and move into Part Two of the book.

M. Sounds good.

PART TWO

PUTTING TOGETHER
A VIABLE CAMPAIGN

CHAPTER 8

Some Reality-Check Questions

"The future belongs to those who believe in the beauty of their dreams."

Eleanor Roosevelt

So, at this part of your journey, you've decided that indeed women are qualified to run for office; all your innate and acquired skills are easily transferable; and you personally feel up to the task, because you want to contribute what you can to your community, state, or nation. Well, if that's the case, it's time for your first reality check. It's so important to do that now and then!

If you've gotten this far, you will probably pass it with flying colors. If not, better to find out early on that you may not exactly be suited to run for or hold public office, but you would be an extremely valuable volunteer. Either way, welcome to the next step—addressing your personal readiness to run. To judge your readiness to run, I recommend you ask yourself the following questions: **Can you *quickly* answer the question "Why do you want to run for office?"** This will be important to answer *without thinking* for two reasons. First, it grounds you and keeps your goal in sight. Second, you will be asked it literally a million times or more, so it needs to be part of you well-thought-out and memorized stump speech.

- **Do you work and play well with others?** Politics is a team sport, and passionate debate a vital part of "the process." As we mentioned earlier, debate is the way we find good laws that can stand the test of time and sustain a strong country. So, my friend, if it's always your way or the highway, go run a business, but not my country or even my library! In business, you can be the CEO of a company and personally direct its trajectory as you see fit. You may have to worry about a Board of Directors, but you will always have more freedom in what you do than you would in politics. Government is all about finding consensus or compromise we can all support.

Now, if you're wondering exactly what traits or qualities mean you *can* work well with others, here's a suggested list. If you say, "that's me" to most of them (and your best friend or trusted associate agrees with you) then you probably are someone who works well with others, whether as leader, teammate or subordinate.

1. You are a good listener – you don't prejudge based on your own bias.

2. You don't interrupt others, giving them time to fully present ideas.

3. You debate ideas, not personalities, and recognize the importance of separating the two.

4. You show respect, not disdain, for your opponent, and his beliefs and opinions.

5. You are willing to work toward win-win solutions— meaning all can at least "live with" them.

6. You accept blame when warranted and share victory when earned.

7. You never take credit for another's ideas.

8. You complete your part of a project on time and as assigned.

9. You routinely "go the extra mile" in what you do.

- **Can you clearly articulate your political philosophy, and recognize how it may impact others?** Cutting funding that would shut down a rehab facility would be an example of how a single decision often impacts many on a local level. A national-level example would be unfunded mandates (a federal law or poorly thought out regulation that requires compliance at a local level without any provided funding) that can deplete budgets and/or drive businesses elsewhere. We've seen it affect builders, small businesses, and the workforce itself.

- **Can you conceptualize and accept the very large amount of non-visible and non-glamorous work that goes with the job?**

  ☐ daily paperwork

  ☐ phone calls to help constituents

  ☐ meetings

  ☐ long hours

- **Can you raise money?**

  ☐ Do you have multiple groups of contacts from multiple sources to fund you? It costs a lot of money for a campaign, and self-funding is not usually the answer

  ☐ The benefit to your campaign from fundraising, besides the obvious monetary one, is that when people give you money they are invested in your campaign and want you to win. They will, therefore, also go above and beyond by offering non-monetary help. They may even bring in third parties to help you if they recognize a need or an opportunity. Remember, you don't have to know everyone who helps you or donates to you.

  ☐ But they do have to know about you to care! So, reach as many people in as many ways as you can, and encourage them to spread the word if they believe in what you are doing.

- **Can you speak in front of a crowd?** Don't freak out over this one. You probably already have done so:

  ☐ At a PTO meeting

  ☐ At a town council meeting

  ☐ At a church meeting

☐ At a scouting event

☐ As a room mother addressing a class

☐ At a Friends of the Library meeting

- **If you haven't spoken in front of any kind of crowd before,** or are afraid you are currently "in the rough," here are some tried and true practices that make it easier. I highly recommend joining Toastmasters, getting some coaching, or watching the preachers on TV. From the TV preachers (whether you approve of the genre or not) you will see how they use cadence, body language, inflection, etc. From Toastmasters, you will learn poise and mastery of your subject matter, and have multiple chances to practice, practice, practice. A personal coach should be able to teach you all those things.

Feeling comfortable during a speech is a must for convincing people that you possess the necessary "gravitas." To do that, you must know your subject matter and truly believe! The natural emotion that shows through with true belief can be very convincing. Then practice in front of a mirror to get even better. Better yet, record yourself on video or on your smartphone. Then play it back. You will be surprised what it sounds like, and probably make a few changes. Practice in front of everyone who will listen. Speaking skills are typically not innate; they are learned. The best speakers have put in the practice time.

Now that you've answered these questions honestly, and to your satisfaction, you're ready for the next step: mounting a campaign. We divide that into several areas. You need campaign staff: a mix of paid staff and volunteers. You need materials that clearly communicate your message to help voters recognize you. You need to acquire data and someone who can interpret it for you. You need volunteers to walk door-to-door or work in the campaign office distributing resources such as brochures, yard signs and buttons. But most importantly, you need a plan. We are on our way to that. It will all come together. We promise.

Your Campaign Will Be Unique

Here's the thing to remember about this section of the book: we can tell you what you need in the way of an office, in the way of a staff, and in the way of materials, but *we can't* tell you how to *run* your campaign day-to-day with the same detail. We will have to stick with the broad generalities, which most of you, unless you have already run for an office, will still find enlightening. Why? Because we don't know *you*, and we don't know the issues that are important to *your* community—probably the issues that compelled you to run in the first place.

For instance, we don't know *your* campaign manager and we don't know *your* volunteers. You might have someone in mind for social-media manager, for instance, who would be so good at that job, she/he would be able to do it at a presidential campaign level. Someone else reading this book might be thinking, where am I going to find a social-media manager? You may have the most meager of budgets, while someone else appears to have piles of money. So, each campaign will be different, based on the money raised, the number of paid staff and volunteers, the numbers of brochures you have to send out, the engagements you secure, and the media coverage you receive.

Something that can make a huge difference in any campaign is the level of sophistication in your tracking of the multiple streams of information you receive. We've learned that your best software is probably the typical off-the-shelf consumer vs. anything developed exclusively for you. This is because volunteers (or even staff) are most likely already at least somewhat familiar with it, cutting down training time. You will, however, likely need someone experienced at defining what type exactly is needed, and who knows how to implement it to reach as many voters as possible, record their profiles, and keep track of voter trends.

Many campaigns over the years through incredible feats of organization, scale, and shareware (free software) have proven that underdogs with lesser war chests can triumph over those that are better funded. This illustrates a word to the wise. **Don't complicate your life any more than you must at such an important time.**

You can ramp up the communication exponentially by adopting a few consistent social media habits as a candidate; have a good strong social media director on staff to guide you, and from the very beginning incorporate the data you gather into an easily accessible system (such as Twitter hashtags). Time spent early on this can mean a world of difference. In fact, it can be the difference between winning and losing.

With so much potentially on the line, we recommend that you be judicious in your choice of a social media manager. Thoroughly check references. Ask how she or he sees themselves and their role in the campaign; make sure that their references prove that they demonstrated that in the past. And make sure it aligns with what you want as far as results.

Campaigning is a very fast-paced reactive experience, often like a roller coaster ride, and no two days are EVER the same. The "campaign plan" is a loose framework that needs to be tweaked often to respond to unexpected circumstances. The adrenaline can be addicting. That's probably one reason why professional campaign workers are driven to go from campaign to campaign, traveling across the country to wherever their special skillset is needed. Working together, we have identified the differences in what people *think* goes on while campaigning and what is the usually altogether different reality. We hope to arm you with exactly what to expect so that you can really hit the ground running with confident enthusiasm.

With that said, this may be part of the reality check. If you need predictability and consistency, you may want to think twice about politics. However, if you are comfortable with shifting gears on the fly when needed, campaigning and holding office can be the thrill of a lifetime. You will be both challenged and fulfilled.

We are arming you by teaching you the PRINCIPLES of running a successful campaign whether it be for the local library board, town council, mayor's office, state legislature, national Congress, or president of the United States. These principles will always be the same. The intensity and scope will be what is different. That's all.

It's simple, yes? We hope you are saying "yes" here because it really is. And as we have been saying since page one, if you are a woman, you are already uniquely equipped. The bonus? If you can run for the library board, you can also someday, when you're ready, run for the higher offices that await. One is a microcosm of the other.

CHAPTER 9

Do It In Steps

"You get strength, courage and confidence by every experience during which you must stop and look fear in the face...You must do the thing you think you cannot do."

Eleanor Roosevelt

Start in your own community. Look for a local news source that is neither biased nor opinionated. In this day and age, we are so used to reading blogs we have to remember that they are "opinions" and not "just the facts." Any good decision requires *all* the facts. That is, no doubt, why you see the better legislators reading multiple newspapers.

Is there an issue that has bothered you, such as a proposed highway going through your town? Or are you passionate about education or literacy? Start by going to a few meetings of the Village Board, School Board, or Library Board. You don't have to wait until the next election to become involved. Start going to the meetings to get the lay of the land and develop a real understanding of the situation.

Remember Kathy Ryg, going door to door with her mother, Sheila Shultz, as Sheila campaigned for Cook County Board? Well, actually, it was Kathy, her sister LeeAnn, and Kathy's two-year old daughter, Karyn, who was wearing a tee shirt emblazoned with "Vote for Nana." This type of family involvement grew from all the home-exampled civics lessons, discussions, and community projects which prepared the next generation for the torch that is inevitably passed. As Kathy puts it:

"My first personal major involvement of local change was with the regional school board. We bought a house in a particular neighborhood partly because of the good schools that were available. When I read the local newspaper regarding the release of property tax bills, I found the district number on our tax bill was different from the local school district, and that our kids, as well as a small group of neighbor kids would not be going to the school district we based our purchase on. We had been misled.

I assumed it was a mistake, and went to see the regional superintendent of schools. He very nicely assured me it was not a mistake, and educated me as to the options I had: hiring an attorney or "fighting" to redistrict our home and the small group of affected neighbors on our own.

He explained I would need a petition with a certain number of signatures and I thought "Heck, I can do that." I had been volunteering for others so long, I knew how to get signatures for sure. Then I would have to present the petition to the regional school board, get it on their docket, and attend their quarterly board meeting to make my case.

That was the process. So I did.

Right before our scheduled hearing there was a similar boundary dispute being heard. They had all kinds of attorneys and presentations; but lost their argument. I, on the other hand, had shown up with a lot of passion, a bunch of 3 x 5 cards, and my husband. We made our case, and ironically won a boundary change.

Well, maybe not so ironic after all. I believe direct involvement and passion can accomplish a lot, but I'm not altogether sure that's what carried my argument. In truth, it all came down to money. The previous case's school district could not monetarily/budget-wise succeed without the requested student population and the tax dollar shift proposed. Ours could manage it; so, in our case, we prevailed." [20]

(**Editor's Note:** This is another example of why knowing and following the process is essential to succeed in politics. Without collecting signatures and getting on the docket, she could not even have presented her case.)

Kathy would go on to serve as a Democratic member of the Illinois House of Representatives, for the 59th District of Illinois from 2003 to 2009, continuing after retirement to act as a respected voice for organizations that were important to her, including the statewide advocacy group "Voices for Illinois Children."

Community involvement is another good way of entering the political arena in gradual steps. It is a good idea for a number of practical reasons. The first is it gives you a great understanding of how things work in a governmental environment. When you step forward in community involvement, the people in your district/state see you as "their voice," much as they would with a candidate. In this way you've created a history with them that can carry you forward. Realistically, if you want to discover for sure that political office will suit you, you may as well put a toe in the water by taking a stand on an issue that is important to you.

When you do that, you are building a resume that will have credence and soon give you standing as an already seasoned veteran. That is so very important in voters' minds as they make their decisions. Don't worry that it could ever "hurt" you. Political experience is valuable, and voters can discern between the man or woman who is experienced politically and those who are essentially "lifetime politicians." The former usually grow with experience, but many of the latter unfortunately "settle" for past laurels earned when they really took care of their constituents, came to work with the heart of a servant, and made them proud back home.

---

20   Kathy Ryg. Interview with Maria Rodriguez, December 6, 2017, Mundelein, Illinois.

Okay, we think we've covered the various ways to effectively get started. With those caveats and inside tips in place, let's talk about an actual campaign—the run that will be different every day, different for every office, and different for every person. And that's the *normal* you may expect, and hopefully welcome!

The General Overview

After having finally made a decision to run, it dawns on you that in spite of your bravado, you are (probably) a novice, and not sure of what to do next. Don't worry; everyone must start somewhere! So, let's start with a basic overview of what's ahead in the way of goals, work, and execution, and expand on these things as we go along.

The very first thing you must do as a candidate, is download the "Candidate's Information Packet" from your state Board of Elections. This packet contains frequently updated rules for every election cycle. Missing a deadline for something that must be done or not following specific rules for filing documents such as petitions can knock you out of the race before you even start. *This is so critical we can't stress it enough: before you do anything else, obtain the "Candidate's Information Packet."* Incorporate all the deadlines into your own personal calendar and into the main calendar for the campaign office. Check the packet frequently. It contains all the requirements and general information for each aspect of the campaign.

Next, talk with others experienced in your area and in the prospective office for which you are running. Based on those conversations, decide if you need a campaign manager. You won't need one for the lower offices such as village clerk or a seat on the Library Board; you but will for the higher ones—perhaps even for Mayor.

More than in any other arena, I would say that the rule of thumb for campaign staff is "Hire slow, fire fast!" At the local level, you are probably not hiring a campaign manager from the well known or veteran campaign staffers, but you will likely find a good volunteer who thinks like you and has some experience working in local campaigns. That is the kind of person you need to work as your campaign manager. It may be worth delving into what to look for in a campaign manager here: someone who can see the big picture and keep you on track. You will be placing your ultimate trust in your manager, so choose wisely.

CHAPTER 10

Hiring Your Campaign Manager And Other Specifics

"Whether women are better than men I cannot say— but I can say they are certainly no worse."

Golda Meir

We're certain that Golda Meir wasn't talking specifically about campaign managers here, but we thought it was a good reminder that men who are likeminded and can take your campaign to a high level should be considered as well as women for spots you have available. They might be enormously helpful, in fact, as they bring the male perspective, just as women bring the female perspective. Actually, the first time I ran for mayor, my Campaign Manager was my neighbor, Mike Lyman.

The campaign manager you engage for your local election run doesn't have to be someone who has worked on local campaigns—but does need to be a strategic thinker. With that said, having someone who has won has benefits. A winning experience brings with it all the necessary relationships with vendors, media, other elected officials, etc. (As a side note, in local elections, you may see a couple of people running together as a "slate of candidates" using one campaign manager.)

The campaign manager typically puts together an overall campaign plan which includes your mission statement, spells out what must happen (your goals) and a strategic plan to get there (your strategies and tactics). *If you are running for higher office, you will want to hire someone who has a proven track record at that level.* They bring a level of knowledge and professionalism to the campaign that adds gravitas and credence to you as a candidate. Usually they work for an agreed-upon monthly fee, and often are promised a "win bonus"—meaning they get a big check if they get you over the finish line

Bare Bones First? Yeah, Right!

Once you have identified volunteers or paid staff who will draw up the plan and prioritize tasks to get going, everyone gets busy to get the campaign going ASAP. And it does happen all at once—this is where you DON'T go in steps! You will feel better once things are in place, but don't actually wait until they are to begin making connections or asking for support. In running for higher office, it felt like drinking from a fire hose! Unfortunately, I lost some support because I waited until the campaign was "in good order" to contact certain people. Some of them had already committed to other candidates.

You need a website, pictures of yourself and your family, your reason for running, and your basic platform (the three issues identified in your stump speech will get you started on your platform.) The first time I ran as mayor, a friend of mine said, "You need some pictures. Grab a couple changes of clothes and we'll take a bunch of pictures at a couple of spots around town." We ended up using a picture of me near our historic bridge looking out into the distance. Worked fine.

For local office, it doesn't have to be fancy; you just need to have some pictures to use on your own material and to provide to the media. Media will want your brochures and media material sent to them digitally. Make sure you *ask* each one about their preference. They will see that as respect for them and their job and remember it.

Once again, technology has made this part so much easier than it used to be. Even for higher office, you no longer have to hire a photographer. I have seen some great headshots taken from someone's smartphone. Same with video. Putting a quick thirty-second video saying why you are running on your website and other social media, including YouTube, can build your support base exponentially.

Your Brand

What is your brand? Campaigning is selling others on why they should spend their vote for you. So, as you are setting up the campaign, you need to identify or create a logo (in this case, how your name will appear and be printed so that it is both clearly recognizable and memorable.) A cautionary note, when designing a logo for your campaign: make sure it is designed to be enlarged for signs and reduced for business cards and stationery. Each version of it must be clearly readable at whatever size you need.

You also will need a slogan, typically a phrase that is catchy, memorable, and that inspires votes for you. Over the years there have been some great ones, and there have also been some real "doozies" that can be either easily misinterpreted or misconstrued; so be sure you test yours out on a few people to make sure they will be understood the way you mean them! Everything you do should advance you toward your goal of being elected.

For instance, here are a couple examples that stood out to us for different reasons—some good, some bad. The following slogans actually worked:

- "I Like Ike" (1952), and "I Still Like Ike" (1956) – Dwight D. Eisenhower Presidential election.

- "Who But Hoover?" Herbert Hoover Presidential Campaign (1928)

- "Happy Days Are Here Again" – Franklin D. Roosevelt Presidential Campaign (1932)

- "It's the Economy, Stupid!" – William Jefferson Clinton Presidential Campaign (1992)

- "Sam's the Man" – Liz's Dad used this slogan when running for an office on the Navy Base—not exactly national office, but he did win, and it shows that slogans are important for any campaign!

In our list of the bizarre slogans below you can see that some are silly puns, some are based on their names, and yet others are innuendo. Take a look at these:

- Thomas Dewey used the same slogan to run against FDR in 1944 and Truman in 1948: "Keep the Ass Off the White House Grass." He lost both times.

- "All the Way With LBJ" raises an interesting question from 1964.

- "Get Clean for Gene" is a not too subtle reminder that in 1968 the establishment still regarded long hair as inappropriate and beards as suspect.

But our all-time favorite is actually a "response slogan" from the 1964 Presidential race. Republican Presidential Candidate Barry Goldwater used: "In Your Hearts, You Know He's Right." His Democratic opponent, Lyndon Johnson's supporters responded with: "In Your Guts, You Know He's Nuts." Still makes us laugh every time we proofread that sentence.

Remember, however that slogans, no matter how good, are only one part of your brand. *All* of this is your brand—who you are, what you stand for, the three main issues of your platform, etc. Your website, your video, your printed materials should all echo each other and the basic tenets of your campaign. If it doesn't work in concert with everything else—it's the wrong thing, whatever "it" is.

Materials

You need to decide what materials will work best for your type of campaign, and make sure they coordinate with all other aspects of it. Although social media is the growing trend, and offers exponential value for your effort, you still need some print media. Try to get references for specifically political printer and design media, rather than an all-purpose vendor. Local is also a good thing for convenience in all aspects. Oftentimes, lower office campaigns combine resources for economy of scale.

I think most candidates will agree that campaign materials are *crazy* expensive. Yet, you need something that will quickly let people know who you are and what you stand for so that they will be compelled to vote for you. This is especially applicable to giving material out as you say hello to people at train stations and other gathering places.

The old-school way of campaigning always involved a **"palm card."** This was similar in size to a "door hanger" that would be full color on both sides and fit in a number ten (letter size) envelope. The candidate could advertise his or her platform on one side and personal details, etc. on the other side. (*Note: by law a disclaimer as to who paid for it MUST be visible on any printed piece of campaign literature. The font size can be tiny, but it MUST be there.*

Whether there is a newer "greatest thing" than the palm card changes from day to day. Ask your campaign manager for an opinion on the best methodology and materials. When I ran, I found I liked something slightly smaller, more the size of a baseball card, (sometimes called a **"prayer card"**) because it could not only discreetly tuck into people's pockets, it could also be tucked into an envelope with a donation request and sent to any number of databases.

Yard signs are another staple in the campaign arsenal. Some people think these are incredibly annoying, but they are *effective*. Here are a couple of tips, though, regarding those signs. Choose as few colors as you can be comfortable with; each color costs additional money per sign. That may sound petty at this point, but as you get into the campaign and see how fast the money goes, you too will be a believer in saving it where you can! Also, if you are campaigning in an area with snow, *don't use a white background*; people can't see it from the road as they drive by.

Bigger versions of the yard sign (called 4x4's) are effective on the corner of a busy intersection. When you are talking to friends and family, ask them if they know of anyone who owns a business in a high-traffic area that would showcase one of these signs.

Direct Mail pieces are typically for higher office or for contested local races. When I ran for Congress from the 8th District of Illinois, each direct mail piece cost the campaign $11,000 to print and send. Knowing what they cost, I now make a special effort to read the different ones that come to my home. Part of the campaign plan is to strategize how many mailers will be needed, and a timeline for when they will be sent. **Word to the wise**: the "arrive by" strategy is no longer election day. It is now the day before early voting starts. Talk with experienced campaigners in your area...hopefully you will find that advances in desktop publishing and printing will have driven down printer's costs. But the point remains, they are expensive. Accurate estimates go a long way toward stretching the war chest.

Bulk-rate mail vs. first-class mail can be a real dilemma. Bulk-rate is cheaper, but not nearly as reliable as first-class mail. So, you will need to both plan early and print early if you use bulk-rate mailing. (The post office has a two-week window for delivering bulk-rate, unlike the quick delivery and predictability of first class or priority mail. As a result, you will never know exactly when within that window your bulk-rate pieces will be delivered. Take that into consideration when you are doing your planning.)

You will also need **campaign stationery in several forms**: letterhead with matching envelopes, postcards, donation request forms (again, very specific language MUST be visible on the form. Details are in the candidate's packet and the states' Boards of Election are very serious about the rules.)

You should also have **note cards** for thank-you and other types of notes. Again, try to estimate carefully how many you will need. Try to use multi-purpose shapes and designs; for example, a note card the size of a half sheet of 8-1/2" x 11" paper with your logo at the top can be used for thank-you or other notes, as well as for invitations or event details. The waste in this "materials" area that is usually seen at the end of a campaign is obscene.

Which brings us back to **social media.** We really feel that social media may be the key to leveling the field among millionaire candidates and those who are good people in need of support to win. The 2016 presidential primary election was historic for many reasons, but the Bernie Sanders campaign offered some especially interesting lessons. He raised a boatload of money asking for just $27.00 per person. He also developed a simple but concentrated grass roots organization using a groundswell of volunteers and social media.

Regardless of your opinion of Senator Sanders, learning about his social media campaign would help any candidate. As luck would have it, a couple of his staff members wrote a book that we highly recommend. Published in 2016, it is titled *Rules for Revolutionaries*, written by Becky Bond and Zack Exley. In later chapters we give you more reasons why this is a compelling book.

CHAPTER 11

Build A Database of Supporters

*"Never doubt that a small group of thoughtful committed
citizens can change the world. Indeed, it's the only thing that
ever has."*

Margaret Mead

Once you have the campaign decisions made, you can begin to identify support. This isn't brain surgery. It's actually very simple: start with
friends and family. This is how you begin building your base of volunteers. As exciting as it is to run for office, it is also profoundly humbling.
The support you receive both before election and while in office is a debt
you can never repay.

I remember when I ran for Congress, it felt like we *all* ran for
Congress. These people put themselves out for me in countless ways.
Several years later, I am still in awe and full of appreciation. Most of your
close family and friends will have been involved in your discussions about
throwing your hat in the ring. Hopefully they get something from that
experience too—knowing someone who is running for office can be like
saying "The quarterback is my brother." They are still spectators, but they
engage in the sport at a higher level.

For both local and higher office campaigns, start by contacting
everyone you know, and asking for their support. I started with a letter
to the people I knew personally (some called this the Christmas Card
list database.) Tell them why you want to run. Give them a glimpse of

your three issues. Then ask them for further support in connecting you to *their* networks.

How will they do that and how will it help you? They would do it any way possible. Some send out a personal letter, though most these days send an email to their network (often simply their address book) telling people that they know you, trust you, and would like to see you elected. Some offer to host a meet-and-greet to introduce you, usually a "coffee" held in their living rooms, though some might host a larger gathering at a local restaurant.

It's a big deal for them to make time to do it and put themselves on the line for you. There are ways to help them. If they send personal letters, make sure the postage is paid for by the campaign. It can also be helpful and handy to offer a prewritten message that they can quickly tailor to their own taste. Prewriting a template for letters, emails, or endorsement quotes is very common in a campaign, and very helpful when you ask someone to take time to write about you. The busier they are, the more they appreciate having something started that they can slightly adjust and send off. Also, that way you can provide the accurate campaign contact info as well as a link to your political website.

They can also ask for support for you from their *friends in many ways other than financial.* The volunteer army that you can call on is nearly as important as the "cash on hand" to any campaign. If your friends want to just urge their network to consider volunteering their time, tell them that you are looking for campaign volunteers *in every capacity,* from clerical to phone bank to door-to-door, or even simply driving around and dropping off yard signs. Including the link makes it very easy for the friends of friends to go to your website, learn more about you, and then sign up as a volunteer, a donor or both.

The link to your website is not just a nicety. It is one of the most important ways to build your base. Always remind supporters to include it and point out that you've sent it along with your suggested message. When anyone they contact links to your website to volunteer, they automatically go into your database. They can be (and should be) refined later as to volunteer or donor or, hopefully, both. Then they can be further designated as a volunteer for "door-to-door," "yard sign," "office," or any other category such as "weekday" or "weekend." The setup of this type of system very early in the campaign may seem like something you want to put off until you "have time." Doing so, however, would be a major mistake. The ability to have these cross-reference entries handled automatically is worth its weight in gold.

Website—Coordinated with Facebook, Twitter, LinkedIn, Instagram, Pinterest, etc.

Along with capturing information, your website also disseminates information, and is a source for further action. For example, when someone signs up to volunteer or to request weekly campaign updates, you then reply to their signup with an automatically generated thank-you email, telling them you will be in touch to see in what capacity they would be most comfortable working for your election. Their email address is automatically added to the database.

If even a fraction of the candidate's networks, and a fraction of their networks volunteer, you have your first layer of volunteers, and even possible staff. Remember, the end game here is to get the most people to vote, and make sure that they vote for you and not someone else. Believe it or not, those two things often require separate strategies. You would be surprised by how many people forget to vote or sincerely think their vote won't be missed. You must tactfully make them understand that is simply not true—some of these races really do come down to just a few votes. It is worth repeating often that "every vote really does count."

I remember continually urging everyone to vote in one local Long Grove Village Board election, even though it was "only" a midterm election. The race was somewhat contentious, so I knew every vote would be important. One of the Trustees narrowly won by eleven votes. The following weekend, one of my neighbors said, "Oh shoot, I forgot to vote…I meant to do that, really." It made me cringe thinking about the narrow margin.

Building a solid grass roots base, (which is fundamental to ANY campaign) is an exponential deal. One of my favorite lines was, "Tell ten friends to tell ten friends." One congressional campaign even flat-out asked people to consider taking election day off as a vacation day so they could be available to drive voters to the polls!

And They're Off & Running!

Although the campaign itself has actually started with securing and implementing her packet of information, it won't be considered by most people to be officially started until the candidate has publicly announced her intention to run. The announcement can be as big or small as you (the candidate) like, but typically it is a bigger deal when the office is higher up. Lately, we are seeing more and more candidates announce by video on their Facebook page.

Once announced she has to get herself on the ballot, and that of course requires getting her petitions signed. Getting the required number of signatures to secure her name is a task aided by volunteers from the database, which is hopefully growing daily. The number of signatures required is different for each office; and is typically tied to a percentage of people voting in the previous election. A couple of specifics to remember: the signers must be registered to vote within that person's district. Check within the packet for any further additional rules.

Liz thought I should remind people that collecting signatures is a little different than asking for a vote. At train stations, for instance, when you are asking people to sign, you can actually say to them, "Now this isn't a promise to vote for this person. You are simply helping them to get their name on the ballot. How you eventually vote is totally up to you."

Finding the Votes

Walking door to door is incredibly effective but lots of candidates don't do it...probably because it takes stamina (and comfortable but still stylish shoes.) Since there are only so many hours in the day, as the election draws close volunteers typically walk door to door to advocate for the candidate in his/her place—which is not quite as good, but still very effective. Campaign strategy data typically details which parts of the district will have the most votes. When I ran for mayor, we identified dozens of neighborhoods, but discovered that 85% of the votes were in just thirteen of them.

The County Clerk's office makes available a wealth of information, from printable versions of the previously mentioned State Board of Election's Candidate Packet to voter information regarding which registered voters actually voted, and sometimes even if they pulled Republican or Democratic ballots in the last primary. Check state by state since some primaries are different, and even those rules may change from year to year.

In Illinois, we don't have to be registered with a party to vote for its candidates in the primary, but we do have to declare out loud which party's ballot we want. So that's how they can not only tell if they voted, but whether they pulled Democratic or Republican ballots in previous primaries. The information generally goes back for several years. They also have giant maps detailing each district, county, or precinct. The campaign office soon begins to look like a war room with all the maps on the walls!

Even in local elections, the effort put into walking door to door or contacting each household can directly influence how close the election will be. The tighter the election becomes, then, the more effort is required. Typically, a group of volunteers divide up the important territories and put together walking packets that include a small version of the map highlighting all voting information for people living along that route.

A volunteer takes his or her packet and walks to each door, attempting to talk with the resident, ask for their vote, and ask permission to put a campaign sign in their yard. *They then mark on the sheet if the person is a supporter or not.* Sometimes individual volunteers offer to walk at random times through a campaign but typically the staff coordinates a Saturday morning "all-hands-on-deck" event offering coffee and doughnuts as they pick up their packets, and pizza when they get back a few hours later. (Lots of pizza gets eaten in a campaign!)

Walking door to door is a key component of the "ground game" and I've known some political operatives who were so diligent with this that they could predict the local election within two points. Kind of freaky, but great!

During the last few weeks of the campaign, volunteers are needed to reach each home and offer to answer questions about the candidate, and once again ask for the vote. With technology changes, by the time you read this book another new contact method may have come along! For instance, when I ran for Congress, I remember there was a thing called a "dialer" which is an interactive web-based tool. Who knows what the next big thing will be—but there definitely will be one.

Also, in the past, the campaign staff typically had a space donated by a supporter where they could set up several laptops for "phone banking." The laptops, also donated, were loaded with a script for the volunteer, and phone numbers for specific parts of the district. This was very efficient because if it went to voicemail it automatically dialed the next number. Today, however, with more and more people opting out of their landlines, there are programs that dial cell phones. Social media also picks up some of this slack.

Building Your Database

Throughout the campaign, you are continuing to build the database that started with your own friends and contacts and grew as you progressed. Typically a spreadsheet, you will use it for multiple and varied queries regarding your base. You will, in effect, have many databases available at once as offshoots from queries of your master.

The database detailing the financial contributions received by the campaign is critically important. Of course, thank-you notes need to be sent to donors. But in addition to doing the niceties, the campaign also needs to *file quarterly disclosures* with the State, which is the responsibility of the campaign treasurer.

Over the years, you probably have seen news reports for one candidate or another having raised so many thousands of dollars compared to their opponent. That info is taken from the quarterly campaign disclosure which is public record. It is also a respected barometer of the health of the campaign. Historically, if you couldn't raise money it appeared you didn't really have the necessary support. It also meant you wouldn't be able to afford to send mail pieces or staff the campaign. So basically, let's be blunt—in the past if you couldn't raise money, you were screwed. Hopefully, now social media mitigates some of the need for extensive resources.

Get Yourself Out There

One of the ways to put yourself out there, get yourself better known, and thus facilitate the ability to raise money, is to attend as many events as possible and speak whenever possible. If you have conflicting events, the candidate attends where she can speak and do the most good in generating support. A staffer, officially called an advocate, stands in elsewhere, or stays behind after the candidate has left the first event.

Going to events is an important part of campaigning and being in office. People want to talk with you one on one—often that is when they make up their mind to support you. At such events you will hopefully encounter both financial donors and people who are willing to volunteer their time and energy in place of funds. Some will do both, bless them! Financial donors are important—but having dedicated volunteers offering their time is often deemed even more important.

Campaigning across the state takes a decisive strategy, or at least it did in Illinois, which is a geographically large state. The staff typically sets up a number of appearances within a stated vicinity, and you stop briefly at each one. As the election draws near, it is impossible to be everywhere, even though you know how important it is. That is why you see candidates show up, give a speech and then leave. This is where you must wear your pragmatic hat. It is not rude to speak and then leave; it is accepted campaign procedure, and your host understands.

CHAPTER 12

Fundraising & Approximate Costs

"Money is always there, but the pockets change."

Gertrude Stein

The cost depends on the size of both the office and the opposition you are facing. It also depends on how much social media is implemented. Actually in use since 1994, this targeted form of campaigning is now also used for fund raising. Supporters are routinely encouraged, sometimes over and over, to give (via an always easy-to-use method) according to their means.

Social media made it possible for younger folks just out of school and living on Ramen noodles every night to support their candidate by giving ten, twenty-five or thirty dollars. It also made it extremely easy for busy executives and foundations to contribute larger amounts. Ease went hand in hand with opportunity and speed of collection to encourage donations from every source.

It is our opinion that social media may in fact be a catalyst in campaign reform with things such as "money bomb" emails asking for donations for a single specific reason by a specific looming deadline. The best news: cost is minimal since there is no postage or printing. Imagine the good that can be done with the hundreds of thousands of dollars that could be saved in each local, state, and national election!

Fundraising for local elections is typically the job of the candidate and again depends on how much opposition is expected. Running at the state or federal level is a different ballgame. There are specific rules regarding financial donations, sponsorship of events and "in-kind" donations such as office space, computers, use of vehicles, or hosted events. That is why the initial candidate's packet that you obtain from your state is so important to get first thing!

Also, in federal office elections there is a cap and further regulations on what one person can contribute. The nice part for the candidate, however, is that if the contributor is married, each spouse may give to their individual limit, combining donations for both primary and general elections at one time and "maxing out" the total contribution. So, to be clear, a maxed-out contribution is one where a single contributor or married couple gives the maximum possible for a primary election, AND money for the general election as well. *Important to remember: if you are the recipient of such contributions and lose the primary election, you must return the general election portion of any maxed-out contribution. Just to be on the safe side, make sure to keep the funds separate.*

Spend Proportionately to the Timeline

Here's a quick example of the kind of "money" problems that can happen because fundraising can seem fairly easy when you first start and get good results. The problem occurs when you then spend so much money setting up at the onset that you are "short" when it's really needed at crunch time. Read what happened to me.

When I ran for Congress, with only a few weeks left until the primary election, I was told I needed to send another mailer, and the campaign, unfortunately, was dangerously low on cash. One night around that time, I was finished with events unusually early and came home to find my husband Ray making spaghetti and meatballs. I had been out all day in the late January weather, and was freezing cold. Entering the warm kitchen that smelled wonderfully like garlic was heaven. But the real warmth came while I was telling him that I needed one more mailing. He was stirring the sauce quietly, and then about a minute later, he looked up with a sigh and said, "Just put it on the credit card. We're in this deep already; you have to give it everything you've got." God bless that man!

I do realize, also, that not everyone can be as lucky as I was with the support and resources that family can or will supply, which is why I give the fundraising "cautions" that I do throughout the book. As I mentioned earlier, each one of those slick political mailings cost a whopping $11,000 to go to just the Republican addresses in the district. Democrats were not even included, being price-prohibitive at that point. As I stood there looking at my husband, I regretted not being more careful allocating money in the beginning. So, learn from my mistakes. *Adopt the mindset that you spend only what you need to!* Plan for the materials you need, the cost to send them, and the number needed as precisely as possible. And make sure it gets on that spreadsheet.

Staying on the positive for a moment with the spaghetti story, the other positive thing that came out of running for Congress was it reminded me how deeply Ray loved me…endlessly discussing issues with me and finding time when I asked him to role play and coach me on responses to issues, then pushing me out the door to be at everything I could attend, never once saying, "I haven't seen you in days." The campaign and election really did not benefit him at all…it was all for me, and he was all in.

I have heard other women, though certainly not all, say the same thing about their husbands. Many husbands or "significant others" take great pride in seeing their wives step out and step up, and see it as a positive. So, don't go thinking running for office means wrecking your marriage or your romantic life. Often it sparks new admiration and deeper love for both of you. The trick seems to be to appreciate that support and keep communicating—no matter how busy you are with your campaign.

Back to the money issue, many campaigns for higher offices hire a professional fundraiser, who typically is paid a monthly retainer as well as a percentage (maybe 8%) off the top of whatever she/he is responsible for bringing in. In federal or presidential elections, this is money well spent.

If campaigning for local office, you may simply need a savvy volunteer or an all-round great campaign manager.

As you can probably see by now, fundraising is not a one-time or a several-week exercise. You and your fundraisers don't just make a few calls, meet a few people, go to a few events, ask them all for some money and then sit back. Fundraising is something that you do *constantly* throughout the campaign. Not once, not a few times, but constantly.

The Ask

Even if you've hired a fundraiser, you as the candidate also make phone calls to major donors. I found that the best way to do so was to plan an hour or two each day for those calls. It's best to decide on a set time so that it becomes a habit and you don't have the chance to talk yourself out of it.

It is also good to write a script that you can use for each call. Yes, you can get *that* nervous on the call that you forget either what you've already said or what remains to be said. You don't have to follow the script word for word, but it will keep you on track and help you cover all the basics. Then tell yourself that you are going to do this for the allotted time; and remind yourself that with rare exceptions, responses aren't personal!

Some people are going to say "no"—lots of people in fact—and for a lot of different reasons. Some people have already committed to support others, so that their contribution budgets are spoken for and exhausted. Some may only support candidates from within their own communities. Some never take a side during a primary, only during the general election. And yet others may harbor hidden biases that you will never know about. As a result, I found that setting a time and having a script made it feel like just another part of the day, and I wouldn't get into a funk when I heard several "no's" in a row. When your calling time is over, stand up and smile!

Although Liz hasn't campaigned per se, her experience in making sales calls was similar. One of her tricks that I would have found helpful is that after you experience a string of no's, make it a point to call someone whom you know is always friendly to you and glad to hear from you. (Yes, your mother counts.) Just the change to a "welcoming" tone of voice on the phone will pick up your spirits once again.

Also, don't attach any emotion to the amount of the donation; you shouldn't assume the amount given means the same degree of sacrifice to everyone. Giving one hundred dollars may have the same effect on one person's budget as giving one thousand dollars would on another's. So, don't project your ideas of money, or circumstances, onto anyone else. Let them be the judge of how much they can give and show your sincere appreciation through the tone of your "thank-you" for *any* amount. I remember getting a check for twenty dollars from Alice Terrell, a member of my husband's *Lion's Club*. Alice was about ninety years old, and I knew how important twenty dollars was to her or to anyone living on a fixed income.

For a congressional or any other higher office, you may be given a list of donors from a supporter who is currently in office and has a relationship with those people. They are usually the people or organizations we talked about who deliberately budget a certain amount of money for supporting political candidates. It seems obvious that you should make it a point to call them or to schedule a meeting to discuss why you are one of those candidates worth supporting. Beware: if you're new to this, it can be intimidating, and since there are so many tasks needing your attention, it becomes easy to procrastinate. But *this itself is actually the more important task*; and here's why. That money is already budgeted and if they don't give it to you, they will give it to someone else. In addition, if you don't contact them, or even contact them much later than is expected, it is a slap in the face to the one who referred you.

To the uninitiated, it must seem an unbelievable thing that you would ask people for money, but believe me, there are people that are just waiting to be asked. In fact, one time I was given the name of a *major* donor by my state senator. I arranged to meet the potential donor for lunch, and as we chatted, I thought the conversation was going very well. Towards the end of lunch this man said to me, "You know, the first time the Senator had lunch with me to ask for a contribution he didn't get it, because he never *asked* me for the money." I remember nervously looking down at the table and thinking to myself that, obviously, this must be the time to ask.

It was the first time I'd done anything like this, but I took a deep breath, looked him in the eye and said, "Well, that is why I'm here. I am asking you to contribute $10,000 to help me communicate my message and get elected." He told me he would be talking to his accountant and that I would hear from him. A few weeks later I received a $10,000 check.

Asking for support, financial or otherwise, takes practice like everything else. It also takes a mindset that you are asking for money to put toward "a good cause"; you aren't asking for money to go buy shoes and a new car! Without sufficient funds, you cannot compete and/or communicate your message. Also, and this is important—remember, when people contribute, they are invested *emotionally* as well as financially. As a result, you also draw in *their* network, because you can rest assured they talk it over with their friends, and you need all the networks you can get.

Although individual requests for donations from large donors are a must, so too are broader events such as fundraisers. Fundraisers are a very good idea because they offer you a chance to talk with people and raise funds at the same time. Typically, you have a volunteer or staff who coordinates the event, with a checklist put together so that food, drinks and campaign materials are in place from the start time. Ideally there would be a volunteer with nametags and a registration ledger at the door, along with a simple "recommended donation" basket. Make sure the registrations include phone and email, as well as names. And (this is important) *have a separate list for already elected officials who turn out.* Elected officials are routinely recognized in opening remarks—thus the need for the list.

You can also have additional ways of fundraising at the event such as raffles and auctions, either silent or live. Hopefully those items for a sponsored raffle or auction come courtesy of your supporters, and have been recorded for campaign reporting purposes. That way you can provide a variety of different fund-raising activities within the event itself, making it both more festive and profitable.

Talking about the fundraising made us realize this is another perfect example of how qualified many women are for the things that will be required to enter the political arena. How many of us have run fundraisers for our church or for some other worthy organization? Quite a few, I daresay. (That was Liz's sentence.) That means you are not only capable, you have been practicing!

Private coffees, which are meetings in local homes where the host has invited a dozen or more people to meet you, are another way to get to know people. These coffees are especially good when running for local office because you really get a chance to meet a lot of different people in an informal and friendly atmosphere. While you may not want to specifically ask for a contribution then, it is customary to have a basket prominently placed near the door in case anyone *wants* to contribute. Make it a *big* basket. And put a bow on it! You want people to see it. This is not the time to be shy.

Internet As Fundraiser

Aside from the fundraising calls, one-on-one meetings, coffees and bigger events, another important funding piece is internet-based fundraising. Your website, as we said, is used both to disseminate information so voters get to know you, and as an important tool in collecting information on supporters and their contributions. No matter what office you're running for, you should have a button on the website where people can contribute. And make it visible—that means appropriately large, and colorful enough to attract attention. (Note: it should never be close enough in tone to a main or background color to blend in and be "lost." Never make a donor work hard to give!)

The large donations are encouraging, but the smaller contributions we talked about earlier are often more important, even if getting them involves more work. The 2016 Sanders campaign was a perfect example of this in action, as were both the Obama campaigns. They each made a big deal out of supporters' giving even under thirty dollars. By encouraging smaller but plentiful contributions to the website, they pulled in a lot of money and developed very strong grass roots campaigns.

One of the ways candidates can encourage smaller but plentiful contributions is through "money bombs." As mentioned earlier, money bombs are timed emails sent out to raise a certain amount of money by a certain date, often to fund one particular thing needed in the campaign. The purpose for the money raised is usually shared in the email to supporters, and they are encouraged to give, even if only a small amount. Not only does it raise money, it strengthens the "emotional" tie of the donor to your campaign. They are truly involved in its success by giving more than once.

Since the details for collecting and accounting for the money are critically important for ANY campaign, along with filing papers to register the campaign with the State Board of Elections, you must establish a campaign bank account. The rules for how to do this are specifically detailed in the candidate's packet that we talk about so much. (You will find a list of addresses, websites, and phone numbers for Board of Elections offices in every state in our "Resources" section in Part Four.) It is *very very very* important that anything involving money is done meticulously and with complete transparency. Whoever handles the money needs to be a very thorough and detail-minded person, because messing up there can be criminal, punishable at least by a very large fine, or even jail time. Enough said?

Executing the Campaign

Once you get to this phase of the journey to holding office, you are starting to get excited because this actually looks like it may become a reality. You should feel good about things! We said that the most important, and thus the first step, was obtaining your candidate's packet from your state Board of Elections. We assume you've done that and laid out all the deadline dates on both personal and campaign "war room" calendars.

Then obtain the needed signatures, plus several extra in case you need to disqualify some. Follow the rules about signer eligibility "to the letter." Hiring an attorney to go over all signatures to be sure they are in complete compliance is money well spent. You can be bumped from the ballot if you don't follow the rules. It happens, as in the lesson Barack Obama taught Alice Palmer in 1996. It is one of the most well-known stories demonstrating the importance of following the election rules. An Illinois senate seat was going to be vacated by incumbent Alice Palmer in 1996:[21]

Evidently Alice decided she was going to retire, so community organizer Barack Obama decided to throw his hat in the ring. But as the election got closer, Alice regretted her decision and started collecting signatures. Obama challenged not only her petitions but the petitions of *all* his opponents. http://www.cnn.com/2008/POLITICS/05/29/obamas.first.campaign/

The CNN article referenced here calls this "Chicago" politics because Obama effectively eliminated his competition. I disagree. All candidates had access to the rules, which clearly state that signatures need to be collected, assembled, and filed in a very specific way. The packet given by the Election Board as a guide for the candidate specifically details the procedure—which in my mind, makes it fair game to bump anyone who doesn't pay attention to those details.

Now, back to you. Once you know what the rules are and how you plan to follow them you must begin to develop a stump speech. As we said earlier, it will be your new best friend—your wingman during the entire campaign.

A stump speech should be no more than ten minutes long but should include three of the main issues on which you are running. One advantage to limiting it to ten minutes but making it cover three issues (or planks) of your platform, and the reasons why you've adopted them, is it forces you to think in sound bites. This will be a lifesaver when you are asked a question by a reporter.

---

21   Drew Griffin and Johnston. *Obama Played Hardball in First Chicago Campaign.* AC 360: CNN, May 30, 2008. http://www.cnn.com/2008/POLITICS/05/29/obamas.first.campaign/ Accessed June 20, 2018.

If you become known for being able to speak in sound bites, you also will get more coverage on television, because you will be known to make a reporter's job easier. He or she won't have to either "pull teeth" to get information or "shut you down" for the sake of time limits. Giving them exactly what they need, you will be a hero to the press. Even more so if you have something worthwhile to say, and you can make it both interesting and relatable to current events, the town itself, the voters you are courting, etc.

In my experience, the more you interact with the press, the more you will see that they are not your enemy. They are doing a difficult and often tiresome job, with deadlines and ratings numbers to meet. The best scenario for all is one of mutual respect and courtesy, aided by a bit of humor, self-deprecation, and a sincere desire to help the other look good. A free press keeps all our elected officials accountable and, hopefully, honest. It is one of democracy's greatest advantages.

You can also use the same sound-bite principle to answer questions from constituents. It will keep you on message, repeating as often as possible the points that you want voters to remember about you. And with every repetition, it will embed those points in your own mind as well.

Speaking of the repetition, one of the things you will find ironic, and we think amusing, is that on the campaign trail you will constantly run into other candidates, including your opponent. They, too, will be repeating their stump speeches over and over again as the campaign progresses, to the point that you will have heard them all so often you will know theirs as well as your own!

Campaign Office As a Tool

So, with stump speech now memorized, here are a few pointers for finding the right office space. First of all, it won't be as if you have the option of picking a space from available rentals—far from it. Generally, a campaign office will probably be retail space donated for your use by one of your donors or supporters. It hopefully will be large, and relative empty. Often candidates in the same party running for lower offices can go together in a large enough space to take advantage of economies of scale.

Getting a donated space is a big way to save money for the campaign itself. Our personal feeling is that you take what you can, but if you are lucky enough to have more than one space offered, choose the one with the best visibility from a busy road. It should be large enough to accommodate several desks and at least one large table, and should have:

- *A functioning bathroom* (that you keep fully supplied) or easy access to a common one

- *Either a kitchen or enough room* in a specific area for a microwave oven, refrigerator, and coffee pot with serving supplies

- *Enough storage space* for coats, boxes of paper, brochures/buttons/ flyers and yard signs

- *A small TV*

- *A large sign for the front window* (you want a window so people can see activity and feel free to stop in.)

Staffing

Staffing needs vary wildly between local and higher offices. However, one thing is always true: you, as the candidate, will have to create the right mindset for them. Attitude in any organization starts at the top and filters down. Mindset is important because it creates a feeling of unity in pursuit of your election to office. It helps focus people should they get sidetracked. It can also be inspiring when you all feel part of "something bigger." Remember, staff members differ from volunteers in that staff have specific jobs to perform and are paid for doing so. They may or may not be as passionate as your volunteers—but they should be, if you create the right mindset. Volunteers work for free and either shift assignments as needed or perform one assignment specific to their skills and ability. Mindset and respect unites them all.

Something occurred to us that we think may be important to think about as you form that mindset that will unify your people to support your positions and advance your goals. We mentioned early in the book that conditions in 2016 reminded us very much of conditions in 1968. Like then, we were in a war we did not understand and seemed incapable of winning, and it tested both our mettle and our morality. Civil rights were being denied, even by police. Riots took place in multiple inner cities; poverty was eradicating entire classes of people, particularly the middle class—an erosion that would only get deeper with time. Values of every sort were being questioned. Heroes, though in demand, were in short supply.

Some of your volunteers will be too young to have even been born then. It will be up to you to draw some parallels, so they see how women then too rose up in what was perhaps the second wave of feminism (if you consider the first wave to be suffragettes) and are again rising now in a third wave. For instance, there is a new wave of women running for office and taking on the challenge of resetting both our cultural and political guidelines and mores.

What we found so interesting is that looking back, it has been fifty years since 1968, and the suffragette movement was approximately fifty years before that. And fifty years before that, there was the Civil War when women were called to step up because there were no men around to run businesses; and step up they did. Each major movement seems to take about fifty years to emerge in full—and about fifty years equals the birth and maturity of a whole generation. So once a generation, people—and women in particular—seem to say, "Our generation must do things, change things, and make the world a better place." That lends credence to two famous quotes by two famous women:

> *"The critical responsibility for the generation that you're in is to help provide the shoulders, the direction, and the support for those generations who come behind."* [22]

> *Gloria Dean Randle Scott*

---

22   Quinn, *Quotations*, page 211

"You may have to fight a battle more than once to win it." [23]

Margaret Thatcher

What a time it is to be a woman! You are part of something that is taking the country by storm, and that honors sisters of the past by building on what they accomplished. We are on the cusp of something great, and it will be your job to show that, once again, it is time for women to be heard as one massive voice in one massive movement. Whether homemaker, working woman, or both; whether single or married, old or young, political novice or veteran, whether millennial, gen-Xer or boomer, you can feel it as women who care!

This is always important to keep in mind when you interview and hire staff, as well as when you accept volunteers. They need to be committed to the concept, to the mindset, so they are convincing on your behalf.

For local office, you will not need as extensive a list of staff as follows, but we are including the full-blown list, so you know these positions exist. You will definitely need them all for the higher offices.

- **Campaign Manager**

  ☐ Identifies and articulates your strategy.

  ☐ Raises as much money as possible, in the hopes there will be some left over after the election—because as soon as you win you are campaigning for the next term.

  ☐ Keeps staff and volunteers focused.

  ☐ Often acts as media relations manager if that is not a separate position.

  ☐ Advises you on and often secures speaking engagements.

  ☐ The campaign manager will be your "go to person." He or she will simultaneously act as your harshest critic, best friend, overseer of scheduling, and spin doctor. Make sure you respect him/her and

---

23   Quinn, *Quotations,* page 218.

can work together 24/7 without wanting to pull your hair out. You also MUST be able to trust his or her discretion.

☐ Note: when hiring a campaign manager, check every reference. Ask the applicants for the position to explain WHY they are the best for the job, and ask for their "number of wins" as well. Some of the best will have a reputation that precedes them because they are well known and move from campaign to campaign. I speak from experience here. The times I thought I was too busy to check references I found myself dealing with multiple problems as a result.

- **Social Media Manager**

  ☐ This may be someone entirely different from your press secretary/ media relations manager. The social media manager will be a vitally important role and demands its own slot. Good and often posted (but not TOO often) social media can, as we mentioned, make or break a campaign.

  ☐ Make sure to make it perfectly clear that any postings must be cleared first with either you or your campaign manager. Misspeaks are bad enough, but mistweets and imprudent Facebook posts are out there to be retweeted and reposted forever.

  ☐ Anything coming out of the campaign, even if not from the candidate personally, is nonetheless forever attached to the candidate.

  ☐ Decide, consulting with your campaign manager and social media manager, what online "personality" you will develop to express your desired image.

  ☐ Stick to that personality so you are consistent, AND seen as such, which is important to voters. Remember your brand!

  ☐ Your spokesperson should always have your trust in her depth of knowledge on your positions.

  ☐ Immediate reaction to social media is important.

- **Campaign Treasurer**

  ☐ This should be a trusted – again, I repeat trusted—volunteer who will be responsible for:

  - Tracking all donations

  - Tracking all expenses (of any type)

  - Making and filling all quarterly disclosures as required by state and federal government

  - Tracking dispersal of petty cash to campaign office staff, and accounting for its expenditure and record of approval

  - NOTE: *Always* have TWO signatures on any checks written. This ensures accountability and helps in fraud protection

  - Weekly reporting of Cash On Hand (COH) is probably one of the most important of all reports. COH is considered another barometer of the health and potential of the campaign.

To get the most votes, which is the campaign's goal, you have to convince the most people in an emotional way that you deserve their vote. People may believe you intellectually, but they are <u>way</u> more likely to take action on what moves them *emotionally*. So, keeping that in mind, the campaign raises money to be able to communicate the message on many levels. Identifying cash on hand for the task, as well as a plan for strategic spending to ensure most bang for the buck, is critical, and ongoing

I heard of one congresswoman who used to say, "I grew up being told not to talk about myself and not to ask people for money; now I spend 70% of my time talking about myself and asking people for money."

Another high-level candidate was pretty direct about it, though in a humorous way. He said it toward the end of his stump speech like this, "Now there is good news and bad news about this campaign. The good news is there is definitely enough money for us to win this campaign. (Long pause, then quieter voice.) The bad news is, it's still in your wallets! So even if you left a check earlier, I'm going to ask you to give just a bit more." People laughed; and then surprisingly, they wrote a second check. You gotta love it.

- **Field Manager**

  This position is vital to the "ground game," which despite the rise of social media, is still a very integral part of your campaign. The field manager will work with volunteers to make use of polls/data/surveys, etc. and will:

  ☐ Identify, by region and street, where the potential votes are.

  ☐ By election day be able to predict with reasonable accuracy where you will end up.

  ☐ Analyze voter data available to all candidates' campaigns, and decide where to emphasize which issues.

  ☐ Determine where the candidate herself is needed, and where volunteers can handle door-to-door in her place.

  ☐ Match volunteers to door-to-door areas and co-ordinate timing of the activity.

  ☐ Work with treasurer and campaign manager to secure reliable, fast, and hopefully inexpensive vendor for printed materials:

    - brochures/mail pieces
    - letterhead/envelopes
    - signs/banners/stickers/buttons, etc.

  ☐ Place orders (using only approved copy) so materials arrive in time for intended usage.

  ☐ Make sure materials get to any other field outposts/offices as needed.

  ☐ Coordinate advance team as campaign ramps up. It is the job of the advance team to go ahead of the candidate and make sure everything will be as expected when the candidate arrives. If not, they deliver that report immediately, so adjustments can be made. They also monitor what the opposition is putting out, so the candidate can address new opposition developments or declarations.

- **Volunteers**

You can't possibly be grateful enough for volunteers! They are essential. That's right, essential. *You simply cannot and will not win without them.* Is there an ideal number? No. But generally speaking, the more the better. They are more valuable in many ways than your paid staff and wealthy donors—but for a whole different set of reasons:

☐ They work long hours without pay, often grabbing meals as they work.

☐ They put your interests above their own for the duration of the campaign.

☐ They "talk you up" to their friends, relatives, and neighbors, even in non-political settings.

☐ They do all the "grunt work:"

- Folding and stuffing printed mailers

- Taking phone calls, answering questions, and routing messages

- Making personal phone calls rather than robocalling

- Posting signs in the middle of freezing nights, pounding yard signs into frozen ground

- Keeping all campaign literature on file and reordered as needed

- Wearing visible signs of support and giving to friends to wear (tee shirts/hats/buttons)

- Typing up and distributing reports

- Keeping track of voter calls on various issues

- Going door-to-door as assigned and reporting back on whether people agree/disagree with candidate on issues, and whether they plan to vote for her or not

- Passing on to candidate whatever is requested by voters

- Advising if a stop-by from candidate is needed

☐ Distribute publicity flyers/meeting flyers.

☐ Send out press kits to media: print/TV/radio/online/bloggers.

☐ Monitor media placements candidate receives.

☐ NOTE: Volunteers save you literally thousands upon thousands of dollars—making them every bit as valuable as any donor. When the campaign is over, you want to do everything possible to reach out to thank all those who have helped you along the way. In addition to a general thank you—no matter whether you win or lose—you should:

- Have election night party budgeted and buy food and drink.

- If someone has gone way above and beyond to introduce you to a helpful person, get you a speaking gig, warn you about an opponent's sabotage, or in some other way help you, be sure to mention it with a thank-you. Sending a handwritten note would be ideal if possible; obviously, it isn't always. Perhaps email if there are a large number of volunteers. Anything to make it more personal will be remembered.

- It's also a good idea to include an "Other" column in your database, so that people who help you in important ways, even though they are not volunteers, are included warmly in a round of "thank you" activity. You may even want to invite them to the volunteer party. The important thing is that they do not fall through the cracks and feel unappreciated for their contributions of time and energy.

- If you win, and then have positions for which volunteers or staff members are ideally suited, offer them the opportunity. They've already proved their value and dependability.

Final note regarding volunteers: it is all well and good to say "thank-you" and "I appreciate you and the fine job you did" at the end of the campaign; but you owe it to these hard-working people to also make sure that during the campaign they are never looked down upon by staff.

Not always, but sometimes staff (because they are being paid, or because they may "direct" the volunteers) think of volunteers as the "B" team, and themselves as the "A" team. *Nothing could be further from the truth.* Think about this: *you could run a campaign without paid staff if you found the right trainable volunteers!*

What to Have Available in Your Campaign Office

Now that you have a specific idea of how to staff your office, let's talk about what those staffers need to know. You need everyone on the same page in their support for you. If any potential staffers make clear they don't think the things you put forward are important, do not engage them as staff, or even as a volunteer. The same principle holds true for those who are "overly enthusiastic" because they often tend to "embellish" to try and help the candidate. Sometimes they help her right on to the front page of the Washington Post, the Twitter feed, or Facebook in a way that is more harmful than productive.

At the beginning of the campaign, go over your positions on various issues that are important to your constituents. Make sure a trusted volunteer indoctrinates newcomers as they join the office so they, too, can articulate them. Make any ground rules that you have clear and easy to understand, such as who is *allowed* to talk to press, who is *allowed* to access petty cash, etc.

Position Papers – Ironically, even though they are called "papers" they will be housed on your website's "Position Page." You will face a lot of issues in your campaign. Some will be easy to deal with; others will be more difficult. Here, in no particular order, is a partial list of issues on which you may have to express an opinion or take a position—thus the name Position Paper.

- Any local issue getting attention
- Immigration – let illegals become citizens/or not
- Revenue – government spending vs. tax cuts
- U.S. Debt – cut spending/cut programs/both; and where/when
- Environment – jobs vs. preservation; conflicts between agencies; over-regulation

- Cybercrime – how to detect/prevent
- Military – build up/cut back
- Infrastructure – maintain/upgrade transportation, water, utility grid, etc.
- Small business – tax breaks/loans/fewer regulations
- Healthcare – keep & repair Obamacare or replace
- College – free/pay
- Church – always tax-exempt/not
- Voting Rights – requiring ID/not
- Death Penalty – for/against, deterrent/not
- Abortion – pro-life/pro-choice
- Constitution – evolving/as written
- CIA – topple foreign governments/not
- FBI – national security/privacy
- Prostitution – victimless crime/tool for sex trafficking
- Space Exploration – continue/cut back
- Law & Order – use of crimefighting resources
- Schools – public/private; charter/voucher
- Taxes – viability of service tax
- Women's Rights – equal pay/equal opportunity
- LGBQT Rights – need to legislate/simply recognize
- Sex Education – school/home; age appropriate
- Drug Use and/or Sale – criminal/not; fine/jail; mandatory prison

Now that we've talked about being ready because you've answered "yes" to the qualifying questions, you've hired a staff, secured an office and stocked it with materials and volunteers, let's talk about what you, the candidate, must bring to the table besides your position papers and your stump speech.

CHAPTER 13

You (the Candidate)
& First Impressions

"When I was younger I always wanted to be somebody.
Now I realize I should have been more specific."

Lily Tomlin

Let's get right into it:

- Remember your brand—better to be a bit overdressed rather than underdressed and regarded as sloppy or unprofessional.

- Dress professionally in clothes that fit well. No cleavage.

- Nails polished in mainstream colors.

- Hair that is natural, professionally colored, or naturally gray—and can last all day.

- Whitened teeth (since so many people use whiteners, those that don't can look like they don't take care of their teeth). The point is to look healthy, but not overly made up. Groomed eyebrows are also important. Voters like to look you in the eye and not be distracted.

- Jewelry that is tasteful and not ostentatious: fashionable but not too large, doesn't clink or make noise (including banging into a mic) that could distract from the words you are saying.

- Shoes that are polished and in good repair (no run-down heels.) Have a "don't care if they get ruined" pair for rain and snow/slush.

- A skirt should not be so short that you have to pull it down every time you sit. It can be embarrassing for a seated audience, or even a TV audience if it's too short. A good practice is to check it for problems by sitting down in front of a mirror–so you can see what the audience sees. It's also good to move around in your chosen outfit a bit to see how the clothes drape when you reach for something, bend over, or gesture.

- Work on your speaking voice. If it is high pitched, very nasal, or geographically specific, work on toning it down. And don't screech just to be heard. Remember, when Hillary ran in 2016, opponents were heard to talk derisively about "that voice." You want them to remember what you say, so don't distract from it. *Stop and lower your voice before you speak.* Practice, so you get used to saying your name clearly and effortlessly.

Mannerisms

- Men assert themselves by taking up space. Do the same. Use wide, sweeping hand gestures occasionally, but not too often. At a conference table, spread out your things to take up your full area.

- Don't play with your hair/face/jewelry/pen.

- Cross your legs at the ankles, not the knees.

- Make sure you phone is either off or on vibrate.

- Don't lean in on top of the microphone. If it is the right height, it will pick up your voice. If it isn't, take a minute to adjust it.

- Try not to stand behind a podium. If you are short, you will disappear behind it, giving the optical illusion of "not being up to" the job. Even if you are tall, it is a negative to put a "wall" between you and your audience. You want to be seen as one of them, and as one who is approachable.

- If you must deal with a podium, park your water and your notes there and leave the podium for most of your speech, walking around, talking to your audience from different sides/angles. You can refer to your notes periodically if you like. Walking around also keeps people focused on you. Just don't overdo it to the point that it looks like nervous pacing.

- Practice a firm handshake (web of hand to web of hand) while looking the person in the eyes as you shake his or her hand. One or two pumps should do it; any more and you seem to be holding on too long.

- If you wear a name tag at a conference, always wear it on your RIGHT lapel or shoulder. That way as people shake your hand they can discretely see your name. You want them to remember you, your name, and how it's spelled.

- *This is very important – Make a decision about drinking at events.* If you are at an event, either do not drink, or nurse one drink all night by adding ice or water periodically and only *sipping* when you drink. This is especially true if you are not a regular drinker, in which case alcohol will hit you faster and harder than it will those more used to it, whose bodies have become more tolerant. Without realizing it, you may vary an answer, leaving it open to misinterpretation. And of course, the last thing you want is a picture of you wearing a lampshade as a hat to appear on Facebook. We exaggerate, obviously, but the point is valid. Someone is *always* taking a picture or capturing things on video. *Remember, not doing damage is a lot easier than doing damage control.*

- When you are at an event, try and keep track of whom you meet. One tried and true plan is to ask for a business card and write something identifiable on the back (beautiful red jacket, son at Notre Dame, bald with glasses, etc.) After the event, you can pass them on to your campaign manager, who will have them recorded in the database along with all the others.

- Together, you can discuss how you may benefit from knowing them and how you might be of value *to them* through your connections, etc. Remember one of Zig Ziglar's favorite mantras—and Zig was one of the best salesmen and trainers who ever lived: "The best way to make sure you'll get to the top is to help as many other people as you can to get there too." [24] He even wrote a book about it, called *See You At the Top*. His advice is just as valid today as when it was written. Be generous, treating others as you would like to be treated.

- If you are at a large event with rapid introductions, simply hand the business card to your assistant and he or she will take care of making any notes and getting the information entered into the database.

- Train yourself to be listening as much as speaking. One trick is to make sure to get at least one piece of information from anyone and everyone you talk to–especially the coat check attendant or other people many candidates ignore. You never know what you will hear that will show you a potential political ally, donor, or volunteer. Such information may give you a perspective on an issue that you may not have thought of. Everyone has a story—and a circle of influence. Let them know you don't think it's "all about you." Because believe us, it isn't; it's all about them. The hardworking honest people, not the politicians, are the glue that holds this country together and need to be represented.

- Let your real character prevail, not who you think a candidate is expected to be. Most (okay, many) people can spot a phony a mile away. Just make sure that the real character that you show is your *best* self—not your "cranky, overtired, talked-out, not-up-for-it" self. People you meet while campaigning have a snapshot in their mind of who you are. So be gracious, even when tired. They expect to see the best you, not a you that "phones it in."

- Don't be afraid to show feeling if something moves you. Emotions show you as human, and that's important for voters see—but be sure they're appropriate emotions. For example, anger is appropriate when faced with injustice, but out of line if it's simply because things don't go your way. Empathy, appreciation and respect are always appropriate. Always keep both the current situation and the end game in mind.

---

24 Zig Ziglar. *See You At the Top,* 1979, Pelican Publishing Co., Inc. Gretna, Louisiana

Getting Elected – Your Full-Time Job

Yes, it's a full-time job, even if it's a part-time office! But you already suspected that, didn't you? Time and energy are both finite, so you must spend yours on the things most likely to help you get elected. That's a simple principle, but like many women, there may be a tendency for you to multitask and do all the things you usually do. That makes it a control issue. Get over it! There won't be time. If you have a family to tend to, order groceries online and find a dry cleaner who will pick up and deliver. Delegate what other household chores you can. That's another reason why you spent time "preparing" your family when you included them in making your decision to run.

If you are single, widowed, or divorced, you still have a life to juggle—so you, too, should delegate what you can, and have the dry cleaning picked up and delivered. What may at first look like very frivolous expenses turn out to be very wise investments, giving you that most valuable of commodities—time. Bank online. Get your nails done professionally and learn a speech at the same time. These are just a few suggestions and examples of adjustments you can hopefully make.

As the candidate, you are rarely in the campaign office. The one exception would be a highly confidential weekly campaign meeting where the candidate and selected staff sit down to go over what has been done in the previous week, what fires were put out successfully, what still needs attention, and what is on the schedule for the following week. Usually it will just be you, your campaign manager, your treasurer, and your social media person. We caution you to make it a confidential meeting because if it should leak out how much money you have, or what your ongoing plans are, that will give your opponent an unnecessary advantage. And that's obviously something you never want to do.

As we said, you will rarely be in the office. Early in the campaign, as you are accumulating signatures for your petitions, you and some volunteers are at various train stations by 6:00 AM every morning, asking for signatures and shaking hands. Then you move on to any other place where you could find a group of people to sign the petition. Those early days typically go from early morning to late evening. Who are we kidding, they *all* go from early morning to late evening! That's because every possible minute should be used to meet people. The number of people you meet directly correlates to votes. The staff and volunteers are using the office during this time, and it gives supporters a place to get answers, material and yard signs.

Spending Your "Candidate" Time During the day

- **Dialing for donors:** Even if you've already scheduled time to call major donors during the day, if you have down time it is wisely spent on making calls during those extra minutes. Some candidates prefer to have a driver for that very reason. They do not look at scenery, they make phone calls.

- **Walking door to door to ask for votes.** Once areas most likely to vote for you are identified, don't take them for granted. All politics is local, and people really want to be asked for their vote.

- **Your scheduled events** (parades, festivals, church/school happenings/library events that promise to draw a crowd). Your campaign manager and you decided they were important enough to get on your calendar. Don't skip them. Show up with a smile and the attitude that you would rather be there than anywhere else.

- **Town-hall meetings** to meet voters and hear what is most important to them. If they are at a town hall meeting, they want to know that they're heard.

- **TV, radio, internet interviews** – Political internet and cable stations, like the topics they cover, are very reactive. Although they too need to fill air time, just like major networks, they are more agile in their programming. You therefore have great opportunity to get your message out. It pays to be attuned to sudden controversies that come up in the political arena, so you can get yourself on one of those programs to comment.

Wherever you go, always bring your clear, concise, valid and relatable message, and find a way to get that message communicated. Be willing to answer questions, give a stump speech, pass out literature, whatever it takes. Eventually you get them to vote for you by:

- Listening to their concerns and empathizing (not necessarily agreeing.)

- Getting their contact info and following up on their concerns, or having your office do so on your behalf.

- Telling them what you will do for them, how you plan to do it, and asking for their vote. Don't, however, make promises that you cannot keep. Promise them that you will explain your reasoning.

There is something else to consider that has always given women an "innate" edge. That is their understanding that the culture in which we live dictates the conditions in which we live and causes many of the problems that we face.

With that in mind, here's the difference in a nutshell between men's approach and women's. Men see themselves primarily as the solver of issues; "Got a problem? Don't worry, tell me about it and I'll fix it for you." Do they eventually make the connection between the culture and the problems it breeds? Of course, but the key word here is "eventually." Men don't always think of culture first as *the thing that needs to be changed.* Women "innately" see a bigger picture. If we are faced with a problem, before we fix it we want to know "why" it exists, so it isn't replicated. We want to get to the "why" of the issue from the get-go. Of course, practically anyone would who had heard a three-year old ask "why" a million times a day! You automatically learn to think in terms of "why."

History shows that from the very beginning of our country, women have intuitively changed culture, usually *while* solving issues. If you want some excellent references for this concept, check out a book by Cokie Roberts, of broadcast fame, called *Ladies of Liberty*,[25] in which she illustrates the many influences, cultural and otherwise, the earliest first ladies of the United States had on our young country as it moved forward. Taken directly from letters, it reads almost like a novel. That is a particularly

---

25   Cokie Roberts, *Ladies of Liberty*, 2008, William Morrow, New York, New York

effective technique to illustrate that once the common enemy, which was England, was defeated, the country's leaders had to crystalize what the new independent government would look like. This was the very beginning of our system of debating different perspectives to arrive at a solution that all could live with, and in addition, would stand the test of time.

Another good reference that illustrates this principal is *Twenty Years at Hull House,* [26] by Jane Addams. She was the first American woman to win the Nobel Peace Prize and today has one of the largest and busiest expressways in Chicago named for her. Chicago's other expressways are the Kennedy, the Eisenhower, the Reagan, and Veterans Parkway—to illustrate the esteem in which she is held in her home state.

A part of Hull House stands as a museum today on its original site. It is connected to the University of Illinois at Chicago and is testament to the vision of providing help to underprivileged women being exploited in sweat shops. They did not have the needed alternative skills allowing them to escape that fate, but they could learn them at Hull House. It also undertook helping children exploited by a lack of child labor laws and health codes. It helped upgrade an entire city that had raw sewage from homes, hotels and shops, along with drainage from the stockyards, freely flowing down the streets because it had no curbs or sidewalks. She instinctively knew the culture must espouse different values before vulnerable people's conditions could be improved and eventually elevated to a satisfactory standard.

Why are we giving you the names of these reference books here instead of just putting them in the Resource Section? Because we want you to understand deep in your heart and in your very bones that **this is not a new concept**. Women have been at the forefront of social change from the days of the caveman, or for our purposes, from the days when George Washington's mother taught him not to lie. Yes, that was hundreds of years ago, but that's the point. Women have been seen in so many primary roles

---

26   Jane Addams, *Twenty Years at Hull House*, 1998, Penguin Twentieth Century Classics (Original Publication Date of 1910)

over the years that it's hard to keep track: you must stay home; you must go to work; you must defer to the man; you must be head of your household.

But one thing never changed. And that was that no matter how they were seen, no matter what "primary" role they had, they seemed to see the bigger picture. Most cultural change in this country that led to social improvement was driven by a grass roots movement. And most grass roots movements in one way or another were started by women! Doubt that statement? Take a look:

- Female nurses during wartime – Florence Nightingale

- Hull House – Jane Addams

- Suffragette Movement – Susan B. Anthony, Elizabeth Cady Stanton

- MADD – Candy Lightner

- Environmental Awareness – Rachel Carson

- Special Olympics – Eunice Kennedy Shriver

- Red Cross Disaster Relief – Clara Barton

- Substance abuse treatment – Betty Ford

- Breast Cancer Awareness – Nancy Reagan, Betty Ford, Susan B. Komen

- Equal Rights for Women – Betty Friedan, Gloria Steinem, Bella Abzug, Marlo Thomas, Maria Shriver

There are many more for you to research and be inspired by. You will be amazed by their stories. And of note, each of the movements above was inspired by or had as its catalyst a personal experience. When something happens to women – they DO something about it.

A perfect example of such action is Candy Lightner, who started **Mothers Against Drunk Drivers (MADD)** after her fifteen-year old daughter was killed by one. Until that time (1980) nobody, and we mean nobody, thought twice about driving home after not only a few, but after many drinks. The culture had to be changed. Attitudes had to be changed. And Candy Lightner did it.

Eunice Shriver, who started the **Special Olympics**, was acutely aware of the lack of activities for the mentally challenged because of her experience with her sister, Rosemary. Each of these movements occurred because a woman understood the connection between cultural acceptance and norms and the ongoing condition of the world, the country, the state, the town, and the block where you live.

These are the issues that we care about, *not in place of* issues like jobs and the economy, but *along with* jobs and the economy. Use your own observations and experiences to make cultural issues part of your platform and you will have an edge over the many men who don't "innately" provide leadership in all the same cultural and lifestyle areas women do. I hope that doesn't sound like a reverse-sexist comment; it is simply the fact of the matter. Hopefully, as women find more and better places at the table, so will men find places in *those* all-important areas. But for now, let's remember and exercise our "cultural awareness" edge when we are candidates.

Now here is something we find ironic. Despite talking about these strong women, and noting how strong women are the "accomplishers," we are still faced with a question (believe it or not) that men don't usually face because they are *expected* to be strong—and that is this: when presenting herself to the public as a candidate, should a woman be "soft" or "strong" in demeanor, attitude, and use of language.

Maria answers this way: "I think that as a woman you want to be seen as knowledgeable. It's not necessarily a *hard* approach; you just state the facts and back them up. Just out of college, I worked for a woman named Louise West. She was famous for saying, "You can say absolutely anything to anyone as long as you say it with tact." I watched her in many difficult situations and never forgot the lesson.

"You find, with practice, that it is possible to disagree with people in a firm way that is not offensive. You learn the lesson that as soon as you get emotional, you are losing the argument (or debate) and as a result, you learn some different and very effective strategies, especially when the discussion gets heated.

"Keeping your cool and knowing when to say a few sentences then shut up and let it hang in the air can be unsettling to your opponent. I think for women, our emotions are our strength. They allow a depth of understanding and/or perception even in the most difficult situations. However, emotional *displays* such as ranting or screaming are never good. If you get emotional, you have lost the debate. The trick is control.

"Again, many of us practice this at home all the time. Raising teenagers definitely provides practice in debating with an irrational opponent! In retrospect, my debating skills have grown measurably over thirty-six years of marriage. My husband is a strong-minded person and so am I. Consequently, we've had some pretty strong conversations. We don't swear at one another or throw plates, but we have no problem either making a point or disagreeing with each other.

"I think that's a healthy thing that's an outgrowth of maturity and practice. I also think it prepares you for the debates you will encounter both in running for and being in public office. Politically successful millennials have compensated for what they lack in life experience by identifying a mentor who can guide them as they make their way through inevitable minefields.

"When you're running, you will be faced with how to react to your opponent. And you'll probably be either falsely accused of something at least once or have your words taken out of context. I think most people go into the campaign vowing to run a clean campaign but inevitably some mudslinging occurs. This is nothing new. The rhetoric and nasty comments by our founding fathers toward their opponents would curl your hair. It is the nature of the political beast. All in all, stay as positive as possible, knowing that once people are committed to a candidate, often they won't pay attention to any negative thing said about that person."

Let's get back to more fully exploring what traits, characteristics, inner beliefs, etc., women have that make them ideal candidates in today's world—a world beset with fears, hatred that shows itself as bigotry, blame enough for everyone but oneself, and a general confusion about what's right and what's wrong. As more and more people look at the country under these conditions and ask what's wrong with it, women have two distinct opportunities. The first is they have an ideal opportunity to step up and show they are aware of all these conditions, and secondly show how they are qualified to address them. If she can adequately articulate this, she gives voters deeper reasons for electing her. Consider these facts and observations:

- *Women are generally acutely aware of gray areas.* Although they see black and white, right and wrong, they also see nuances where men may not. A perfect example would be when a man sees an underperforming employee and understandably elects to fire him. In the same situation, Liz and Maria each remember hearing that a woman often would see that same employee, intuit that he may simply be in the wrong job, reassign him, and watch with pleasure as he shines in his new role.

- *Women are typically relationship driven.* They like to learn the other person's reasons for doing or not doing something, feeling that understanding another's motivation will make the relationship better through empathy. They generally offer advice when asked, listen when challenged, and consider the possible validity of criticism. They find the good in their opponents, try to encourage that good over any "evil," and give praise when due—either for deeds or character. (We believe this is called "bipartisan.")

- *Volunteerism has programmed them to step up when needed,* consider the good of the majority when looking for solutions, and search to find the solution that is right, not just easy.

- *They, like men, are creative when needed, pragmatic when called for, and traditional out of respect for people or institutions of value and honor.*

- *Very importantly, they are NOT paragons of virtue* who have never ever made mistakes (ever seen the show *Orange is the New Black*?) but they are generally people whose default position is to try and do the right thing. They apologize when necessary and stand their ground on principles that should be inviolate. They are trustworthy, for the most part, and they usually keep their promises and their word. While not wanting women to sound either like boy scouts or faithful canine friends, these virtues, nonetheless are often mentioned in connection with women for a simple reason...they exist in them.

- *They are aware of the value of goods and services.* Many women spent years and years squeezing the household budget. Others worked to pay off student loans or start their own business. They value people over money, but recognize the need for and proper use of money to achieve an end. These women are frugal, but generous as well. What a long way we have come from the movie portrayal of women as ditzy gadabouts who don't have a clue how much things cost. Our vision is much more realistic these days!

These are the values passed on from good mothers to their children generation after generation; and they have never been needed more than today, when so many women are head of households. Mothers lay a solid foundation for life. It is no coincidence that individuals considered to be major successes in this world in business, sports, finance, education, and even acting often thank their mothers in award-acceptance speeches.

In accepting his award for MVP of the 2013-2014 season, basketball star Kevin Durant clearly and emotionally thanked his mother for being the force she was in his life. For setting the tone for her household. For believing in his ability to overcome sorrow and adversity. For mentoring him as to which values were real and which were fleeting. She made sure he knew right from wrong, good from bad, and convinced him that with those lasting values and perseverance, a better future could be his. And it is. Consequently, it was with great emotion that he mentioned her many sacrifices in helping him rise above and finally leave his early environment. He called her the real MVP.

Stories like Kevin Durant's remind us how women not only lay the moral foundation, but by modeling and enforcing it within their spheres of influence, also affect the cultural climate that reigns. The movements were not always perfect, and were not always inclusive (to our great civil-rights shame even today), but eventually the grass roots movements the likes of that started by a tired Rosa Parks that day on the bus, along with those of women like Candy Lightner, Eunice Shriver and others who shared the same moral compass, have moved us along. The time seems to have come again for women to rise up and stare down the hate and the bigotry that, though often unconscious, is still very real.

As we said at the beginning, this book in no way means to be partisan. We are *all* to blame for the government we get by either not voting at all, or for voting without full knowledge of the people we choose, then sitting back and thinking we've done our part. It's simply not that easy. We must be vigilant and stay on top of what's going on every day around us. Both the elected and the electorate have this obligation, and this privilege.

Again, recent anger and protesting have something else in common with 1968 that bears noting. Both then and now those who rose up were ordinary citizens who had felt marginalized, unheard, and totally fed up. That led them in 1968 (the anti-war protestors, hippies, other protest groups, and women of all political parties) and once again in 2016 (this time the middle-Americans who have lost jobs, incomes, homes, and all security, women of all parties, and most recently student groups) to take matters into their own hands. You cannot deny people for extended periods of time and not expect rebellion of some sort. It is the natural order of things.

Dare we hope that with more elected women in legislatures, governors' offices, and even in the Oval Office, the repeated marginalization and denial of basic rights might not occur? Consider this; the groundwork laid by mothers was internalized and taken even further as most women became mature adults. Some took longer than others to get there—we accept that fact. Some still aren't there yet. We accept that fact also. But the thing they have going, and this can't be stressed enough, is they became adept at quickly and continuously shifting both their roles and their priorities daily. They do so to manage the "big picture" of the households they run, within the framework of their culture. At the same time, they proactively try to elevate that framework by raising the bar in their own families and communities.

In running these households, mothers show us daily that that they are adept at deciding "yes" or "no" to all requests. Nobody has to remind them to do a cost analysis, ROI estimate, or identify a break-even point. They do it automatically--often immediately and in their heads—without consulting any financial wizards on staff. Example: "Yes, you may spend that much on a prom dress, but then you will have to do your own hair and wear the shoes you have. Up to you." And with that type example we also see their ability to teach the reality of budgeting to the next generation. A simple lesson covering mathematics, priorities, pride, and perhaps even a certain amount of gratification denial in service of the end result.

For some reason, we accept that men routinely make these split-second evaluations and decisions, but still are amazed when we realize women do too, and have been for years. It reminds us of the old cartoon showing the famous dancing couple from the 1940's, Fred Astaire and Ginger Rogers. Fred got star billing and all the acclaim as a dancer; Ginger, not so much. Many years later someone showed a cartoon-type picture of them dancing, she in a flowing dress and he in a tux. The caption was something like "Ginger Rogers did everything Fred Astaire did— backwards and in high heels." How many of us have turned to that cartoon for validation! Liz says when she saw it, it was a real wakeup call…one of those life-changing moments when something hits you like a buzz saw on the back of the head.

Mothers also know how to reward an effort and encourage high-level performance as well as any NFL coach. They have systems of reward for good results as motivating as any company's bonus plan. The rewards are merely of a different, more age-appropriate nature, and often involve four wheels and a steering column. The point is that women are familiar with the concept of an appropriate reward for tasks completed or services rendered. A vital part of a rewards appropriateness comes from being something seen as valuable enough to work toward.

Finally, they are especially adept at mediation and conflict resolution. Example: "If you want to use the car Saturday night, I think it's only right to let your sister have it Friday night so she and her friends can go to the movies. You can't have it both nights. That wouldn't be fair." You get the point. It all boils down to "you can't have it both ways" and "it's only right" and one of our previously stressed words: respect.

These women face the same everyday challenges in their personal lives that they would in business or politics, but at different dollar levels and in a different arena. And as the populations ages, the women also are often forced to deal with the additional arena of elder care. The principles behind the solutions are always the same. They are derived from the same thought process and from the same confidence in executing your decisions to effect a solution that you would need in any elected office. In government, however, remember it's not just you acting as a CEO, it's you working in community with others—sometimes *many* others. But the skills never change. They merely expand and contract to fit the situations.

We've all had to deal with the well-meaning but self-centered egomaniacs! Finesse, my sisters, finesse. Better to deal with them as allies than as enemies. Or, as the pundits say, keep your friends close but your enemies closer. You've probably found it's possible to neutralize dissenters by giving them an important job; and they will probably do it quite well. Remember to *keep* neutralizing them by praise for what they're doing, and then giving them something else to do.

This is one of the things in politics that we discussed as being different from a business environment. In a business, you would have time to "coach" a member of your team who wants to be helpful but either "overdoes" it or in some other way gets in everyone's hair. In a political campaign office, you simply don't have that option to coach because things move so fast and usually there aren't enough hours in the day for the things that are, in fact, going right—let alone for dealing with our abovementioned overzealous "helpers." Better to either fire them outright if they're paid staff, or just keep them busy if they're volunteers.

If, however, you're dealing with someone who is always showing up late, argues with everyone, turns in shoddy work, or worse yet, forgets to do the work, your approach needs to be a bit different, obviously. This is real life, and as you follow the "hire slow and fire fast" policy we suggested, that guy is out! Perhaps you didn't hire slowly *enough* in that particular case, or perhaps the person who presented well in an interview was not the same person who showed up to work. Either way, let them go and move on.

After having discussed the positive traits and the negative possibilities, the bottom line in their qualifications is that women, like the animals sensing the coming storms, seem to not only innately know what to do, they also seem to know exactly when to do it.

- Women know when to stick with a movement, or when to leave because it's either no longer valid, or has become unproductive or self-serving.

- They can also usually keep the above from happening.

- Women have the ability to create a snowball effect, and that is perhaps one of their greatest strengths. They are experts at starting with a single idea, based on a strong and personal belief, then sharing that idea with other women in their own networks and spheres of influence. Suddenly it's a snowball gathering input as it rolls. Input that's showing how to best effect change.

- If they don't like something – if they've had enough – women tend to *do* something about it. Then look out, the snowballs roll. We seem to always know when we have, as now, great political theater, but not necessarily good governance.

In January of 2017, we saw this play out dramatically, as huge groups of women protested in several different cities at the same time. It started with an idea a woman in Hawaii had and posted on her Facebook page (that gives us a great illustration of the exponential value of social media). But remember, long before Mark Zuckerberg and Facebook, or any of what we now call social media existed, women communicated ideas through handwritten letters, telegrams, telephones, and then faxes and email. Then as now, the ideas spread from network to network and materialized as peaceful marches in every major city, and even some small towns in America.

The Women's March in 2017 deserves examination for several different reasons. Let's take them one by one. First, they had a great showing; and second, they had a lack of violence. That can't be said for every peaceful march. Unfortunately, in the past, many cases of violence in the streets were *reactions* to peaceful marches, such as in the early suffragette movement. Still, women will not be deterred.

Women knew then, and they know now, how to get it done, and how to get it done right. They don't pound their chests and proclaim how wonderful they are. At least the majority don't! They do, however, accept praise, and are usually visibly pleased; but chest pounding is most definitely not the norm.

Now, for all of you who think these comments about women seem somewhat fawning or sugar coated, get over it. That pushback unfortunately happens sometimes when you make a list of good qualities of people in a designated group. We know that women are not "perfect;" and just like the men, we have our share of idiots. Women are not saints, thank goodness; but they are smart; and they are talented; and they are eager and willing to serve. Let's get more of them into office!

By the way, in the case of the aforementioned Women's March, more than one newscaster compared the scouting, logistics, and execution of the march as equal to or even surpassing the same processes routinely done for a presidential candidate on the stump. No small praise—and no small accomplishment. Women have finally learned not to think small. How cool is that!

So, what are the lessons from all this? There are a great many. Women were fed up, and wanted their voices heard. And they didn't ask permission from the men to speak.

Another thing is that women in their twenties, thirties, and forties, like their mothers before them, were stepping up and stepping out of their comfort zones, marching side by side with the "gray hairs." One of Liz's fondest pictures will always be the one of her daughter marching with a woman old enough to be Liz herself.

It was especially gratifying because the commonality was sisterhood, not political orientation. Liberals marched next to conservatives and old hippies shared the streets with millennials. There were, of course, in this as in any cause, those who will have conflicting views of the march. Some will say that "they" didn't feel welcome, as a result of their stance on various issues. Arguments can be made for and against those statements, but we do not want to get bogged down in such specifics or micro-analysis. The point we want to make by focusing on the march is that women had had enough, and did something about it. Something that couldn't be ignored for either its existence nationwide, or for the quality of its planning and execution. There will always be some dissent/counter-points that exist.

One other thing we found remarkable is that many of the women went out of their way to be there. This was especially important for Boomer women who had been politically active all their lives to see, since many had thought that Generation-X, which is the one that immediately followed them did not have the same recognition of the need for involvement and activism as they did. The march proved otherwise. To give a quick example, Liz's daughter and two friends from Chicago, for instance, were in Indianapolis for a funeral on the day of the march. The three of them decided to rise early and march right there in downtown Indianapolis, since they would miss Chicago's. When the march ended, they changed their clothes in the back seat of their (compact) car and drove to the funeral properly dressed. I have no fear for Generation-X. They are ready to be in charge.

Recapping their experience for us, these daughters born to our generation told us that not a single person they could hear marching near them made the other party, either Republican or Democrat, feel as if they were "the opposition." They came together as one marching unit—smart, caring, confident women with voices and votes that count.

It was a wonderful display of unity across the country. And it seems, at first blush, to have made an impact. But here we must point out something very important: ***When you march, you make a statement. When you're in office, you make the laws.*** Think about that. And think about the great difference between the two. Then, after you march, run. Run for office! You *know* you've been thinking about it. We're giving you the inside scoop on how to do so. And there are other organizations that want to help as well. A variety of them are listed in Part Four's Resources section. You will find that once you put your toe in the water, individuals and organizations will come out of the woodwork to help you.

But we know not every woman will want to run for office. There will be some who want simply to help those women who do. That's actually one of the many reasons we added the Resources section of this book. When women are trying to figure out who to help get elected, they will recognize some of the people running for office just by reading the newspaper either in print or online. But there are also other ways to find out which women are running in your district and state. You can check with your county clerk's office to get the full list of candidates in your area.

Follow the issues that are important to you; try to learn all sides of them; and help the candidate or prospective candidate who most closely corresponds to what *you* believe. For example, if immigration is your concern, you will want to support a federal candidate. Your county board will have no direct influence on that particular issue. If your cause is education, the school board and the county board will definitely have direct influence in your area, so you would want to support a local candidate.

As we said earlier, volunteers are the lifeblood of any campaign. There is much you can do, and so much you can accomplish as a volunteer! Any candidate will tell you, it is a greatly valued service. They simply cannot get elected without a full complement of volunteers.

Nor can they get elected without money! Think about donating, as well. That gives you a vested interest in the campaign and makes the long hours and hard work seem less tedious. It also gives you the satisfaction of being assured that you had a real part in the candidate's win. And believe us, that's a thrill like no other.

There is, as you can see, a seat at the table for everyone. Hopefully, when you are finished reading this book you will not only be inspired to take your first political steps, but also know whether you want to be a candidate or a volunteer. Being either one will move the country forward, and you will have a say in the direction.

One brief note—or maybe not so brief. Politics is something you can both step into and out of, depending on your lifestyle and circumstances. Many women will eventually leave politics for reasons as diverse as they are. Some will stay forever, convinced it's their life's calling. Others will see it as a great way to effect specific change and then leave the arena.

Why are we laying it out like this? Because whatever role you see for yourslf, and whatever length of time you feel you can give to the improvement of the political landscape is up to you. How you live, how you work (or don't) and how you spend your time is a personal preference. And remember, what we all have been fighting for as women, whether Republican, Democrat, or Independent, is the right to be in the game and be a voice at the table!

For an interesting take on this "stepping in and stepping out," you may wish to Google the Honorable Susan Garrett. She now chairs the Illinois Campaign for Political Reform, a nonpartisan public interest group. She is extremely effective, highlighting for instance, pertinent facts in a case regarding political clout's overriding job requirements in a state agency.

She came there, however, after serving as a Democratic member of the Illinois Senate for ten years, and prior to that, serving in the Illinois House of Representatives for four years. Although she was elected as a Democrat, she proved herself to be an independent thinker throughout her tenure. In 2011 she chose not to seek reelection to office, but rather "step out" to work in the non-profit sector. She is an example of how the options are there for you, just as they were for her to step in whenever and wherever you think you are going to be most effective.

Her story also shows us several other things. The first is how many different options you have once in office. Serving on committees as Susan did, ranging from transportation to appropriations, to education, to state government offers opportunities to make a meaningful difference. You may also find that your interests/strengths make you a good fit for your current office, but a great fit for a higher office. Armed with both a clear understanding of that higher office and some established relationships, you can give that campaign an undeniable edge. Finally, Susan has demonstrated how your influence doesn't end once you leave elected office. There are all kinds of opportunities to bring all that you've learned politically to an organization that you care about.

Now for some fun stuff for those of you that like to "dive deep": What happens to you when you run for office?

Life is funny. Even when you think you know exactly who you are and exactly where you fit in this world, running for office suddenly gives you a much broader world view. A person cannot be exposed to the incredible diversity of experience one encounters in politics and not have. We would all worry about you if you had not been affected by what you saw on the campaign trail. You will leave that trail, we promise you, with newly opened eyes.

You will be hearing the most intimate details of people's lives, and putting faces to the issues. They will tell you how much money they earn and why it won't go far enough. They will share family stories about a child who got run over and beg for more stop signs in the neighborhood. They will complain about teachers, doctors, bus drivers, and their bosses, and wait for you to agree with them and tell them how you can help.

So yes, you will be affected by all that. You will be affected even further by the realization that as much as you want to, you can't always help. Eventually you will be able to explain that to them with no personal feelings of guilt.

Maria tells the heartbreaking story of sometimes not being able to meet everyone's needs. Sometimes there are simply problems in doing so. For instance, village funds must be used for essential services and functions, and discretionary funds seldom remain after that. Those that do remain must be used in ways that help a large number of residents, not just a select few. That is very hard, especially if the cause is close to your heart.

So, is it tough sometimes to be in office? You bet! But is it worth it? You bet! Being Mayor was one of the most challenging, yet most rewarding experiences of her life.

And don't forget, they call it "experience" for a reason. It is what makes you mature even further, grow even smarter, and dare even greater. Experiencing the day-to-day reality, you realize that you can handle it, and you grow more confident in your ability to think through situations, make good decisions, and take viable and comfortable positions. In today's world, however, you will also notice things that you will probably find sad or disturbing—and for just a second or two you may wonder if you have made the right choice. Rest assured, you have. Let us tell you why.

There is a growing sense that politics is no longer an honorable profession. Right and left we read about those who have disgraced their office in one way or another. As an honorable woman, you can be a valuable addition to the political process in this country. Keep in mind what we said about culture in this country: it is the women who change it. Other countries seem to have realized that long before we did. Think of England's Margaret Thatcher and Theresa May, Germany's Angela Merkel, and India's Indira Gandhi, among others.

In fact, Susannah Wellford, who helped found *Running Start,* an organization that aims to get young women/girls interested in politics has been quoted as saying:

> "The U.S. has (an) abysmal record on women in politics: As of last Spring (2016) just 20% national level seats (were) held by women, and the local level's just as bad. And although that

number rose slightly this election cycle, we're nowhere close to the 50-50 rates of nations like, say, Iceland." [27]

Her quote above was recently confirmed by the latest PEW study.[28] Given this statistic, it begs the question "What really keeps women out?" Wellford cites several things. Here are the first three:

- fear of public scrutiny

- lack of funding

- concerns that a political career would keep them from having children.

We've covered those three, as a matter of fact, letting you know what you will be facing, that your time will not be your own, and yes, people will be watching and asking about any skeletons in your closet. We have helped set your mind on a path for fundraising, and shown how women can enter politics with or without being married, with or without children, and by the same token, can "leave" politics whenever they choose to refocus on family life as their main concern.

But brace yourself, the fourth and *main* reason Wellford cites is that *"Women simply don't think they'd be good politicians."* [29] That's a big, big problem, and it's exactly the one we're trying to help solve by writing this book. For many years now it seems that women who "make it" in the political landscape have been viewed as anomalies. Well, we agree they are unusual, but they're unusual in that they ran, *NOT* in that they had the skills to run. We want you, too, to be unusual!

Liz remembers reading a piece years ago that said most girls who are bright in math, for instance, start to "dumb themselves down" in about sixth grade (at approximately 11-12 years old) because of the social pressures to "fit in" with their peers. She also read that particular grade/age is

27   Landsbaum, *How to Get More Women Involved in Politics.* https://www.thecut.com/2016/11/how-to-get-more-women-involved-in-politics.html Accessed June 20, 2018.

28   http://www.pewsocialtrends.org/2017/03/17/the-data-on-women-leaders/ Accessed July 17,2017

29   Landsbaum, *How to Get More Women Involved in Politics.* https://www.thecut.com/2016/11/how-to-get-more-women-involved-in-politics.html Accessed June 20, 2018.

the time of a student's schooling when an unconscious shift takes place in the classroom, and teachers start to call on the boys more in class! Hopefully that may be starting to change. It's vital that it does, because actions like that sadly reinforce the idea that to fit in, a girl should remain silent. After all, no other female is being called on. Disturbingly, often when girls call out with an answer, they are reminded to raise their hand. When boys call out with an answer usually no such reminder is given and often their answer is not just acknowledged but praised. We need to make it cool for *all* girls to be just as outspoken as boys.

Hearing about and addressing issues such as the above cannot help but influence your thinking and make you wonder what you can do and how you can help change things. Want a suggestion? Run for the Library Board in your town, and regarding this specific issue, suggest they start to portray math and science as "cool" subjects, and have a science club or math club for the "cool girls" and the "cool boys." Play it up. Watch what happens. Some libraries in Northern Illinois have already done this with success. Why not in your town?

Have some contests as boys vs. girls; then pair girls with boys. Start the conversations that you care about. It doesn't cost much to run for a Board position. Take the first step, then the next, and watch life change. Running for office, win or lose, enables you to not only analyze what you did or didn't do that worked, it also allows you to recognize strengths in yourself. And that strength can take you many places.

Also, you will no longer take officials for granted, now knowing what they have been through, and you will fight with all your might and all your newly made connections to keep the bad apples out of the barrel. After all, that barrel is yours now. Win or lose, you're in because politics is one arena where failure is seen not as defeat, but as a stepping stone. It is not unusual to see someone run multiple times. Abraham Lincoln didn't win the first time either. In fact, he didn't win the first dozen times. Thank God he kept trying!

Finally, there is one other way in which you will also have been changed. You will have gone from being a person with strong opinions who wants to act on them and get immediate results to one who respects the process. You will know that the debate of an issue is just as important as the understanding you have of it.

Think about that for a minute. We said earlier that it is from respectful debate that we get our finest laws. You should now be able to discuss your opinions and listen to those of others without wanting to bang on the table or punch the person you're talking to. You now take time to educate yourself on all sides of an issue instead of going along with the first line of a blog or with what the commentator for one of the highly political channels has been pounding home.

You should be able to smile and say "yes" when asked if you think for yourself. You'll have confidence in your discernment, rather than parroting back something you've heard influential people say. And you should be able to say "no" when asked if you automatically expect that a person who affiliates with one side of the political aisle completely agrees with *everything* the party's other members say. You will be a new and better version of yourself—baptized by fire, tempered like steel.

Maria's Tales From the Trenches – Quoted Directly

The lessons learned through holding office and campaigning in various races, winning some and losing others, have actually changed the trajectory of my life, making me see that I was capable of things I had never dreamed of. My memories are overwhelmingly positive. Especially after such success as being Mayor of my town. Politics also provided some lasting funny and/or embarrassing memories that come to mind now and then.

Perhaps my most *embarrassing* moment while campaigning—since Liz assures me everyone always wants to know that—happened when I was running for Congress against five men in a primary election. I had never planned to run for Congress. I was happy working as Mayor. A couple years into my first term, however, I was urged to run by people I respected who offered to "fill in the blanks and help me with the details" of that kind of campaign. *I seriously suggest much more planning than I did or had for this level of campaign*, but in case you decide to throw caution to the wind, perhaps I can at least save you some embarrassment!

I began to give it some serious thought. I had worked closely with my Congresswoman and was impressed by her early voting record. She was a Blue Dog Democrat, which meant fiscally conservative, putting her in line with my own thoughts, as well as with the district's. Her voting record changed, however, when President Barak Obama was elected. She began voting strictly along party lines. *I liked her as a person, but my concern over some votes grew into reason to challenge her job in Congress.* It's important to be able to separate the two: the personal (I liked her) and the political (I didn't like her votes). I also have had friends disagree with *my* politics (including Liz) but it did not change our relationship; we agreed to disagree.

At that time, the political climate was also changing. She was not the only one to change her voting. Many strong conservatives felt that when Obama took office, the floodgates had opened for a more progressive agenda. That was a perfect breeding ground for a new movement, and it was called The TEA Party[30] (Taxed Enough Already) with strong right-leaning conservatives wanting to be heard. Across the country constituents were feeling unsure of their congressman/congresswoman's position, and were demanding Town Hall meetings to explain their fluctuating votes.

I was only a couple of weeks into my campaign, but I thought I should get a jump on my opponents. So, I gamely suggested that I, even though just a candidate at that time, host a town hall meeting. The event was, by all accounts, disastrous—but I learned a great deal and gained some incredible volunteers from that day. Here's what happened.

I went into that primary thinking I was ready. After all, I had been successful in the mayor's office so far and had developed a reputation for being fair. I was well versed on municipal issues, and had no problem with

---

30   Editor's Note: Yes, it is an acronym, as well as a reference to the "previous" Tea Party in Boston. As an acronym, it means Taxed Enough Already. That's why we have capitalized it throughout the book.

people challenging my opinion or my stand on Village issues. I also read the newspaper and worked closely with state and federal representatives from my part of Illinois. The lesson I learned, however, is that there is a big difference between forming an opinion about an issue and forming a *defensible position* on an issue.

Because I got into the race late and without a formal plan, I relied on others who had volunteered to help get the campaign up and running. I was concentrating on getting the required 3,000 signatures and meeting as many people as I could. At the same time, some of the volunteers worked on putting up a website, necessary of course for a serious contender. The content that was initially posted was in keeping with the traditional GOP stand.

As I continued to develop a deeper grasp of the more contentious federal issues, and my understanding of them evolved, I was not completely comfortable with the sweeping campaign promises. Campaign promises can make a solution sound either black or white, and as both a woman and a Mayor, I had learned firsthand that there is always "more" to any story, and nothing is EVER as simple as it seems.

At the same time, pulling the campaign together and getting it up to speed as quickly as possible, I was pretty busy! *So* busy, unfortunately, that neither I nor my staff had relayed my "evolved" positions to the webmaster. Yep, you can see this coming like a Mack truck, can't you? Let's just call it an oversight with consequences. Talk about being "green."

Fifty or more people attended the town hall meeting that I had thought was such a great idea, and my initial speech went alright. It was basically my stump speech, and although I was beginning to get comfortable with it, I didn't yet know it backwards and forwards and sideways, as I've advocated here in the book. That's how I know you must!

When the Q&A. session began, however, it became obvious we had a problem. As I began to take questions, I realized from the way they were worded and the positions they were asking me about, that we had not updated the website and my "evolved" answers were now conflicting with it. I wasn't all that sure of myself as a speaker to begin with! My mouth was so dry that that it felt like my teeth were sticking to my lips.

Some of my opponents' supporters in the audience seized the moment, which I confess, was fair. I was frustrated and embarrassed as my now conflicting answers were exposed. I was humiliated as I apologized to those who came to support me. They were legitimately disappointed, which was hard to watch. However, they were also willing to stay and tell me what bothered them and offer suggestions to improve my presentation. It was a wonderful feeling to see how they wanted to build me up instead of tear me down. They saw past my poor performance to my potential, which was humbling and gratifying at the same time. And truly, during the whole campaign that was the worst that happened. And it never happened again.

I am sure any candidate or veteran office holder has a story like that. A campaign must be looked at as a marathon, not a sprint. You must cover all the bases (pardon the mixed metaphor) and see small failures as an opportunity to learn. Not only will it save you future embarrassment, but looking at it that way helps you get over the failure. And you will find that people will respect you for that attitude.

So much so, as a matter of fact, that they will often come forward and volunteer to help you. One man from the town hall meeting sent me a list of "deep" questions that helped me get to know myself better, and recognize what I stood for and what I would and would not accept from my own party. I was building my brand before I even realized it. The meeting was fortuitous for both of us in that he became a trusted advisor and remains a good friend to this day. He went on to work on other campaigns, taking his career on a different trajectory than he first envisioned, and eventually becoming one of Illinois' best state senators.

When you push yourself through something that is frightening and come out on the other side realizing it didn't kill you, but instead taught you something, that knowledge gives you newfound confidence.

But I also tell this as a *cautionary* tale. Despite my sensible words now, it took a long time to get over this and get to that newfound confidence—which I needed in order to take strong positions and defend them with gusto. That may be part of the reason for my loss. I'd like to go back to something we said earlier, because I think you'll be able to see the tie-in. When you put a campaign together, it is necessary to be able to deflect controversial or extraneous questions by bringing them masterfully back to the three critical issues you thoroughly understand and have made your own.

It's a way to avoid ever sounding like you are an opportunist who decided to run for the sheer prestige of being in office. Having some thought behind the issues that you can express in a way that even constituents who don't agree with you will understand, shows your intentions as pure. Voters will also see that you are not shrinking back from a fight, but instead are standing your ground based on well-thought-out solid ideas.

I think if I had done a better job of that, the Town Hall meeting would not only have been less of a fiasco but could have been a real bump to my campaign. So it bears repeating that you must know those three issues so thoroughly that you can always find a way to bring the questions back to your stump speech articulation of them.

The thing I really did learn about losing, though, and try to employ in every aspect of my life is that the sooner you mourn your loss and emerge from your grief, the better! I returned after that campaign to finish my first term as Mayor, and then happily serve a second one. Some years later, after my children were much older, I would again run for higher office, that time for Lieutenant Governor.

Let's Raise the Bar

It is unfortunate that politics currently has such an awful connotation. According to Gallup Polls on U.S. Views and Ethical Standards, there's presently a four-way tie for "least trusted professions" in America: lobbyists, members of Congress, telemarketers, and car salespeople.[31] Car salespeople are no less trusted than members of Congress? Really?

---

31   https://news.gallup.com/poll/187874/americans-faith-honesty-ethics-police-re-bounds.aspx

I know many good and honest citizens who step up to direct our country in both good and bad times. Part of the reason to write this book is to urge *more* good people—especially women—to step in and grow the number of "good" politicians to critical mass. People want good leaders. Frankly, they don't really care all that much what the gender is. It's the dedication and integrity that they want returned to political office.

I remember getting an email from one of the shop owners in our Village that actually made me shed a tear. A man who was a registered Democrat was offering to help me, a Republican, write speeches. He said in the email that he wanted to help because he knew I would be fair. See what I mean? That desire for quality and fairness in our leaders crosses party lines at every level from local to national.

I also remember the day Liz Richards called me and suggested this book. She said it could show the everyday woman that running for office could and should be considered. That it was not an "out-there" thought, nor only for people who are political. For me, Aunt Jane, who was introduced in the Q&A part earlier, was the first "regular" person I knew who ran for office. She was as honest as the day is long. It was having her as my model that reminded me that sometimes the best candidates come from the home and hearth.

I was not a politician either when I first ran. I know we jumped ahead a bit ago in our timeline to talk about my "embarrassing moment," but my own first campaign was for village clerk. I stepped up for the first time because my Village needed a clerk, and the time commitment was reasonable at two nights a month. My campaign slogan was "You just met a girl named Maria," a tagline memorable enough that I didn't have to campaign too much. Thank you, **West Side Story**. Of course, there is rarely much competition for the Village Clerk's position! A year or so into the term, a trustee stepped down and in an upward move, I was appointed to finish his term. In the next election for trustee, I was re-elected. Taking advantage of the fact we mentioned earlier that you can run for the length of time that suits you and your life, I served until we purchased a farm and our oldest child was going to high school.

Learning as much as I did from the trustee's job about how the governmental process works, I felt qualified several years later when I was approached to run for the higher office of Mayor. It was in doing so that I had my very first public misstep. Not so bad that it couldn't be overcome; not as bad as the yet-to-come "website incident" that would happen later when I was running for Congress, but memorable nonetheless.

Why am I telling you these things? So, you know that *anyone* who has been in the running for office, *at any level*, has also been in the running for gaffe of the year. Shake it off and keep moving. It's harder to hit a moving target! I shook it off and was elected as Mayor two terms in a row, despite the misstep of my first mayoral debate. Perhaps this is the place to note exactly how shy I had been all my life. Like many people, I was extremely self-conscious, so public speaking was terrifying! I had made a monumental effort to become more comfortable in social situations through college and young adulthood, but it was an ongoing effort. Speaking at small group gatherings such as coffees was fine. But debating was a whole other game.

My opponent was a successful and highly polished retired businessman. I did not, however, agree with his philosophy for the Village, and was confident that I could be a better Mayor than he. But I was nervous going into the debate. After reading his campaign literature, I called my campaign manager in a panic. I told him that the opposition's materials were so good that the average resident would read them and automatically vote for the guy! Plus, it didn't help that I heard he had been captain of the Yale Debate Team. Somehow my work at University of Illinois in Chicago paled in comparison to Yale. I kept reminding myself of why I was running: the ideas I had were needed to set the Village on a better path for the future.

As we took our places, I noticed many familiar faces in the front of the crowd. I was nervous as we started. and stayed nervous as we continued. I was stuttering, using "ums" and "ahs," and not always answering in complete sentences. Finally, I just decided it was obvious that I was neither good at this nor comfortable trying, and it was too late to sign up for Toastmasters! At the end of the debate, my younger daughter ran up, put her arms around me, and said, "Oh Mamma, are you okay? Your face was so red I just wanted to run up and hug you."

As a side note, I didn't realize then just how important the lessons I was learning were going to be to my children. As a mother, we often have the chance to show our children how to handle difficult situations. In this case, she saw me be incredibly nervous and terribly embarrassed, but push on through anyway. Then (in what seemed like a miracle after that debate) she saw me go on to win the election. It was a great lesson for all three of my children to see somebody paralyzed by fear not only live through it, but continue to pursue her dream. Even I was proud of me.

While campaigning, it's important to not take yourself too seriously. Issues, yes; yourself, no. Campaigns are *reactive and in constant motion*. In any campaign you are sometimes either exhausted or running on sheer adrenaline. As election day nears, even the most disciplined candidates say things they can't believe came out of their own mouths. All you can do is laugh at yourself, explain yourself, apologize, and get over it. It makes you more human, which is not all bad, as long as you don't do it regularly. Try to make the best of it by using the sudden attention to direct the voter toward something positive that you want them to remember.

For instance, Liz recalls a time when she had to do just that, even though it wasn't in a campaign. She attended a job fair held in the main lobby of a local college. Completing an informal interview, she backed up to leave but caught her heel on the edge of a step. Falling into the open center space of the event, she landed flat on her back with her feet in the air. She could sense everyone's looking at her and had heard the collective gasp when she went down. So she got up, dusted herself off, smiled broadly, and said, "I forgot to mention, I have grace under pressure. Thanks again for your time."

That was what she wanted them to remember: grace under pressure. She got the job. And when she showed up for her first day of work as Executive Assistant to the President of the local company, he greeted her by saying, "You'll love it here, there are no steps."

Some things though, that happen between you and the press, for instance, are hard to redirect. Remember, it's easier to not do damage than it is to do damage control. For the record, I had no trouble with the press because I remembered a few guidelines I'm passing on to you here:

- **Prime time for gaffes is before or after an event.** You and the reporters are likely just "hanging out" or waiting for your rides. Think of that as the "danger zone."

- Sometimes gaffes can happen with reporters if you think something is "off the record" and they don't. Here's the rule: Unless you tell them something is "off the record" *before you say it,* **EVERYTHING is on the record and can be quoted.**

- Even though the same reporters tend to follow your campaign and you get to know them a bit, **never get conversational or make offhand remarks**. Why? Repeat after me: Everything is on the record unless you say it isn't before you say it.

- **They have a job to do.** That is to capture something that will make their paper or their news broadcast stand out. We believe in making their jobs easier by always delivering the "w's" (who, what, when, where, why) in concise fashion—not by giving them unasked for remarks. Remember: stick to your stump speech.

- **Treat them with respect, and they will do the same for you.** Respect their deadlines if you call a press conference or call them to talk about something. Don't call them right before they go to press. Want to really impress them? Ask each one that you work with what is his/her deadline and what's the best time to reach them with comments or news? It's the equivalent of giving the doorman a big tip. You never have to open your own door again, they are anxious to do it for you.

- **Finally, it is their job to print what you say, not to make sure you look good!** Making sure you look good is *your* job. This is another situation where we know the rules, and if we don't follow them, we have only ourselves to blame.

The Central Plan

Okay, so we've talked about the goal from the 30,000 feet perspective—getting elected. Then we came down to earth and talked about the various components you'd need to win and listed a lot of the specific tasks involved; but again, these are all "components" of something, and that something is The Central Plan! Nothing gets done well without a plan.

It's worth going into a bit of detail here about campaigning for higher level offices, even the presidency, because we think the details of running for national office most clearly and fully illustrate the plan needed to get elected to any office. It also helps you to understand what will be happening if you volunteer for someone who is running for a national office. The plan for "going big" and getting a national candidate elected is largely the same as for local elections: announce, present, mail, door-to-door and modern technology engagement of voters, followed by activity to move voters to the actual polling places.

Your central plan is just that...central to everything, and the "hub" of what you do. It will involve focus on the candidate and will contain the strategies for the main goal: getting her elected. You often start with some opposition research.

As the candidate and her campaign staff look at the competition, aided by opposition research which can be purchased from specialists in that field, they can see:

- the strengths and weaknesses of each candidate
- core beliefs and positions of each
- voting records and accomplishments/failures in getting bills/ programs passed
- popularity/problems with demographic groups
- experience in politics/business/leadership/non-profits
- skeletons lurking in closets
- controversial positions that could be exploited

So, the candidate and staff must figure out how to use this information in the best way. Don't forget, the end goal remains the same: to get elected. What pieces of this information play into the strategy for that? What parts of the reporting do they use, ignore, or neutralize to make it a non-issue. **Note:** To not be surprised by anything the competition throws at them, the candidate also usually buys opposition research on herself/himself.

But as you know, information is absolutely no good to you unless you extrapolate what you need and then tie it all together somehow to get the most from it. We suggest that you look at the research on you (or your candidate) and the opposing candidate in a sort of side-by-side comparison and based on those comparisons, craft a profile that lets your audience see you as who and what you are, as well as what you are not. If you are experienced in areas where your opposition isn't, for instance, list that as a favorable characteristic, disassociating yourself from those without that experience, and standing apart as the "expert" on related issues. Do the same thing when it comes to associating yourself with something that they are neglecting. Point out that you "care about" an issue because you've written/spoken/gone somewhere/done something about it, in contrast to the "other guy(s)" who have done nothing of any significance on the topic.

The point is very similar to having a stump speech. With this information, you can redirect things back to the topics you want to discuss. For instance, in response to a question you don't wish to answer because you're weak on it, redirect attention to something you're strong on by saying something like "I guess I'm simply more focused on the "jobs/economy/unemployment/lack of transportation/gun violence" you have in your state, and I don't always worry about what old Joe/Tom/Kathy does in that area. I know you need more (fill in the blank) and I'm on it, fighting for every one of you."

As we have said in a lot of different ways, maintaining control of the conversation can be critical. You must make sure to project yourself in the way that you want people to remember you, and that must be a way that would encourage them to vote for you. This does *NOT* mean crafting a phony or fictitious character. What it *does* mean is that if voters had a choice of three or four different things to think about you as a candidate, you control which one(s) comes to mind. You help them envision the reality that in fact does exist, but this way it exists with your spin on it!

Your Campaign Pillars

So, developing a message, figuring out who needs to hear it, deciding how to get it to them (via door-to-door, TV, print, Twitter, Facebook, Instagram, etc.) then building a support structure to help you do that, and, finally, getting them to the polls to make sure they vote for you is the essence of the central plan in any campaign.

Those are the pillars around which you build your campaign's foundation and add the steps and resources to execute it. No matter how few or how many resources you have available, no matter how big a war chest, the plan remains the same.

But in a presidential election (don't be so quick to dismiss this, you never know—you might be just the candidate the country needs) you also must deal with the electoral college **votes.** So not only do you need enough popular votes, they must come from states that can help you reach the required electoral votes (currently 270 out of 538.) Why? Because elections have shown that you can have more popular votes than your opponent, but still not get elected if you don't have the required number of electoral votes. You don't, of course, need to worry about this in local or even state or Congressional elections. In 2016, however, it certainly made a difference for Hillary Clinton, and that difference was between winning and losing the election. Al Gore was another example of the same thing in the 2000 election.

Okay so far? Good. Now what you must do is make sure you have your "how" support strategy covered. The "how" translates to both staff and volunteers reaching those people who need to be reached, within both your base and the undecideds. This is especially important if the people reside in what are called the "later" states, meaning the ones whose primaries are neither one of the first four (Iowa, New Hampshire, South Carolina and Nevada) or the eleven that fall on "super Tuesday" (so called because of the large number of primaries held that day). All the rest receive far less attention, and even more importantly, they don't always have a staff member on the ground and in charge.

So, what do you have in a staff member's place? A well-trained volunteer who is "in charge" of carrying out the central plan through phone banks, door-to-door, etc. That's when campaigns become scalable, making use of all their people and all their tools. Local and state campaigns can apply this strategy in the "districts" where the candidate herself will not be appearing.

While the candidate is going door to door wherever she may be at the time, volunteers in places where she can't be act her stead. They all have an individual purpose and assignment: to contribute to the activation of the plan, with or without the candidate's being physically present. TV interviews, free press received from appearances and speeches, social media, phone banks, and coffees all come into play as the plan comes alive. And as they do this in concert with each other, each member of the campaign carries the central plan to the voters by getting out the message of what the candidate believes, what she wants to accomplish, how it will help voters and help the country. Now, you are starting to see how all the things talked about in our overview would fit into a specific plan.

Making It Scalable

Let's talk a bit about how you make it scalable. That ability will be beneficial to local, state, and national campaigns. You can never have too much money or too many volunteer! In major campaigns, in particular, volunteers *are* the campaign—another thing about Bernie Sanders' campaign that resonated with both of us. Remember how we said not to downplay them or give them less credit than due? That's why.

While the paid people with titles (staff) were concentrating on the first several primaries and then on Super Tuesday, Bernie's volunteers began to set up offices on their own. Yep, they just started setting up— and did it before they were even officially on the Sanders' payroll! They just kept figuring things out and scaling as they went. Maria has talked glowingly about volunteers since Liz met her, and now Liz is a believer too. You can't buy or hire that kind of determination and passion! It's the passion that figures the way and lights the path moving forward. Again, in their book, *Rules for Revolutionaries*,[32] Becky Bond and Zack Exley give an excellent description of how this all works. So to dive deeper, pick up your very own copy and give it a read.

Now, do you know how Bernie accumulated so many volunteers to start with? Respect and brains. Respect for the man and his message that was based on the same understanding most women have: that in any movement or cause, basic culture must be changed, not just a policy or two. In addition, staff truly respected volunteers and treated them as equals, even training "super volunteers" to stand in for the staff and train newer volunteers, conduct huge mass meetings called "barnstorms," enroll another batch of volunteers, and start all over again. This is what we are advocating: carrying respect with you as a given, and respecting those to whom you report and those who report to you. They will definitely, in our opinion, respond in kind, allowing you to travel as you need to while they "keep the home fires burning" with campaign advancements on a daily basis.

In the 2016 election, for instance, each candidate had a central message and a plan. Bernie's was to defeat Hillary and then Trump; and Hillary's was to defeat Bernie and then Trump. Trump's was to reach out to the disenfranchised-feeling voters and consequently defeat them both! In all the books and articles we read in preparation for writing this book, an important distinction about the strategies each used to execute those plans was made. Some were successful; some were not.

They all point out that when Bernie was gathering volunteers, Hillary was gathering money. Both are good strategies, but one must ask herself about the circumstances of their use. Which one will be MOST effective under YOUR circumstances is important to know. Bernie didn't

---

32   Becky Bond and Zack Exley, *Rules for Revolutionaries*, 2016, Chelsea Green Publishing, White River Junction, Vermont

have much money to take him everywhere he needed to be and do everything he needed to do, so in his situation decided that volunteers must come first, and then use the volunteers, together with social media, to gather donations, albeit small ones. The success would come from their huge numbers and frequent repeated giving.

Hillary needed to convince working class people she was on their side and working for their concerns. By spending a great deal of her time attending fundraisers held by wealthy donors, was she aligning her efforts with her goal? Perhaps not. It makes for interesting conversation. She felt she needed a large war chest and concentrated on that, perhaps to the detriment of her focusing on seeing all the people she needed to win the electoral college vote.

So you see, nothing in, around, or about politics is "a given." Things of such importance as resources and how you employ them are worth an intense conversation with your entire inner circle in order to get enough perspective on the matter.

Another thing that has to be considered is data itself. How far do you trust it, when do you let it over-rule human advice and counsel, and how do you know how to choose which form of life to believe: raw data that has taken on a life of its own, or human beings that have gut instincts born from experience? That's one more thing to ponder. We want to tell you about each of these political choices/directions so that you can feel confident in your decisions.

First, in amassing volunteers, emails are a good first step, along with press releases, of course. Announce that a member of the Candidate's staff will be town on such and such a date to speak about her campaign and give people a chance to volunteer. Those who respond positively to an R.S.V.P. link make up the beginning of the volunteer database. They received a text to remind them of the event as it drew near. (We assume you have already included friends and family, as suggested earlier.)

At the first meeting in a particular area, it's important to weed out who is just there for the heck of it, and who really is ready to work on the campaign. Perhaps a brief speech stating the candidate's goals and telling attendees how much they are needed is a good way to start. After that is when you separate the doers from the lookers! You have to find a way to gather them (the serious ones) into appropriate groups.

Bernie's volunteers/staff probably looked very much like the limo drivers at an airport at such times as the staff stood at the front of the room with their signs announcing their particular venue and address for holding phone bank evenings. Those who were serious gathered by the appropriate sign as far as being geographically and date wise convenient. By doing it that way instead of having potential volunteers and "the lookers" sign in when they entered, there was some certainly that the people who volunteered had heard the requirements and were ready to work, not just curious.

It basically isn't anything more complicated than guaranteeing that the right message gets out to the right people. So you invest time and energy in acquiring volunteers. Simple enough that anyone could repeat the process. And by being repeatable, it was also scalable. *NOTE:* By the time the campaign was over, 600+ volunteers would have held 1,000+ barnstorms (mass meetings) and made over 100,000 calls to voters.[33]

Why is this, along with having other groups doing door-to-door and advocating for a candidate so valuable? *Because research has shown definitively that the most effective tool in moving voters to the polls (remember, they need to actually vote, not just like you) is not TV, not radio, and not social media, but person-to-person engagement with the voter either door-to-door and face-to-face or by direct contact (NOT robocalling) over the phone.*[34]

Although Bernie obviously didn't win, we feel it's important to point out that what he did was indeed noteworthy. With a staff of volunteers, he came from behind to within striking distance of stealing the Democratic nomination from the presumptive candidate.

Okay then, looking at these various methods of contact, door-to-door is easy to understand, but also easy to fall short with if not careful. You ring the bell, ask if they're registered, have they heard of your candidate and do they

33   Ibid. Page XVII

34   Ibid. Page XIV

know what she stands for, etc. Simple; we all get that. But critically important is to at the same time represent the candidate in a way that the voter *bonds with her vision and goals*. Most important of all, however, in any campaign, is to ASK FOR THE VOTE! It's surprising how many candidates skip that; but ask any salesperson of any product and they will tell you, the most important thing is to ASK for the order.

In talking to the voters, you also find out if they plan to vote and if they need a ride to the polls. (You'd never guess how much providing rides increases turnout!) Then you report each result back at the office to the people who need to know, like the campaign manager, and the people who will update the database.

There is another element Maria points out with which you may be vaguely familiar, but still not know exactly how it works. That is poll watchers, and what they do and how they do it. On election day, these poll watchers are extremely important. Before they ever arrive at the polling place that morning, the poll watcher will have received a list from the campaign office of who (which voters) have not yet voted either by absentee or early ballot. This list is based on the previous couple of weeks' information from the county.

The reason the poll watcher is such an important and timely information conduit is that he or she sits *behind* the election judges and keeps a record of who has voted that day at that particular polling place. She or he also specifically notes who has not yet shown at the polls who had promised to vote, and then contacts the campaign office. The campaign office, in turn, contacts those voters and asks them if they need help getting there. This should be someone detail oriented, dependable, and not hard-of-hearing. Not kidding about the hard-of-hearing requirement! Although the poll watchers are a critical part of any volunteer network, never forget that it is all the volunteers combined that make the difference.

For instance, volunteers are also valuable for telling staff what works and what doesn't when it comes to the tools they are given and materials provided. That's especially true of computer programs, database upkeep, etc., which the staff may not use to the same degree as the volunteers. The volunteers quickly become aware when things are awkward or lacking a necessary component. This goes back, again, to respecting the volunteers, and their intelligence as well as their work ethic.

So, can you see now how what we as women do every day with our organizing skills at church, school, library, non-profits or business equips us to understand these game plans? Just as in those efforts, every day, no matter what our station in life, we basically figure out the message, pick a way to deliver it, recruit enough people to help us, delegate as necessary and practical, and concentrate on following the central goal to achievement. You know how it goes if we have a problem. We find out where and what it is, and if we can't solve it, we call in an expert and ask her/his advice. Boom. Done.

And you know what one of the best things Liz found in the book about Bernie? At the very end, Becky, one of the two authors, validated everything Maria and she have been saying all along:

> "At every barnstorm and phone bank meeting we attended, we found that the dominant demographic was women who had working class jobs, service jobs, and professional jobs such as health care worker or teacher. Their sincerity, and authenticity, their concern for everyone, their down-to-earth professionalism, and their firsthand understanding of the life-or-death stakes of the campaign for millions of Americans helped make Bernie's movement great..." [35]

To that, we say, "Amen!"

One final thought on any campaign which hopes to benefit from the incredible value of social media in attracting volunteers, is to pay attention to the sequence in which each type of social media is used. That can be a crucial factor to success. It appears to us that you must start with the broad-based email, which you ask the recipients to also post on their social media sites as well. Then the field is narrowed via the number of responses to the emails and postings, and a return "welcome" is sent. Typically, those responders are serious and at that point can be reached with further updates through texting.

---

35   Ibid, page 119

PART THREE

YOU WON – OR LOST – NOW WHAT?

CHAPTER 14

Win, Lose, Or Draw

On election day, seeing your name on the ballot, and then voting for yourself is a special thrill. Although there are early voting options, most candidates vote on election day at their designated polling place. It's a good photo op with constituents, and helps temper what can feel like a long day, even though it's a day full of anticipation.

Let's face it, winning is more fun than losing. But in retrospect, you learn lessons from losing. And politics, unlike most arenas, is a place where you are not necessarily diminished in future races because you lost. You are expected to give it another try in the future, using the wisdom gained from previous campaigns to win that next time. That is why, along with closing the campaign accounts and writing thank you notes, you may want to write down what you did right and what you did wrong while it's fresh in your mind. It's a practice that is not only cathartic but can be valuable in future campaigns.

It is also why there is a specific protocol to be followed if you should be on the losing end of the race. You want to leave voters with a sense of respect for you and your post-election actions. It is important to start any election with a good reputation. Whichever way it turns out: win, lose, or draw (recount needed), following protocol differentiates the political opportunists from the servant leaders. For example, only when the race is too close to call, or the number of votes is within the margin of error, is it appropriate to ask for a recount. We stress that it has to be within the margin of error because a recount is a costly process. It requires paid election judges to go through and manually count each ballot, but it can be worth it; sometimes it actually changes the outcome.

Regardless of that outcome, it's best to be gracious. I've been both a winner and an "also ran" in elections. In my experience, voters remember a sore loser or a gloating winner in future elections. The first time I ran for Mayor, for instance, I was the underdog. The night of the election, the incumbent was continually up by a handful of votes. Finally, they counted the last precinct. Knowing that the lion's share of the votes were coming from that precinct offered hope. Suddenly the numbers on the computer screen jumped, and I was way ahead...I had won! Amid great excitement, neighbors, friends, and supporters came over to the house to celebrate. My phone kept ringing, and the voicemail was full. It was a wild time.

A couple of years later, I learned what it was like to lose. Earlier I described my less than stellar run for Congress. When approached by my State Senator to run, I gave it considerable thought and felt I could be useful in Congress, so I agreed, without prior planning or high-level campaign experience. It felt like drinking from a firehose! My folks came into town from North Carolina for the election night party at a local restaurant. Although the numbers weren't high early on, we had high hopes; after all, we had seen this before.

All of a sudden, the numbers were going the wrong way. As that happened I remember feeling sort of numb with a full range of emotions: sadness, frustration, guilt...disbelief...I came in third! I'll never forget getting a call from one of my opponents saying, "I was planning to head over to your party to celebrate with you if you won." How kind. It's funny the things you remember. It's also a great example of how you can be opponents without being enemies.

Watching election results come in can be a nail-biter whether you are running for Library Board, County Board, or Congress. Intellectually, everyone knows that there are winners and losers, but even the least viable candidate holds out hope that he or she is indeed the winner. You couldn't really keep the pace and enthusiasm without being convinced it was all going to be worth it, right?

The protocol for winners and losers following an election is an essential part of the American system. The whole "by the people, for the people..." implies that we AGREE to accept the outcome. Once election results are final, the losing candidate is expected to call and congratulate the winner and then make a concession speech publicly conceding that the other candidate has won.

Losing a primary race can be particularly hard because after conceding that you lost, you are then expected to not only embrace, but work for the winner. The first time I watched a primary candidate that I knew do this, I was astounded. Her name is Kathy Salvi. Not only did she make her concession speech that night, but did so in time for the evening news. Giving the public concession speech following a primary loss is particularly hard. It is difficult to look into the faces of supporters and sincerely thank them for working so hard, and then in the next breath urge them to get on board with "the nominee." Kathy was most gracious in doing that. In a primary race, that's what you promise to do early in the campaign, and no matter who wins, when the election is over you're on the same team.

To emphasize the team approach, the party traditionally holds a Unity Breakfast the next morning. It was there that Kathy presented her check for one thousand dollars towards her former opponent's campaign, so that it was clear to all attendees that indeed unity did prevail.

Kathy became a great friend, and when I decided to run for that same Congressional seat, she and her family offered all kinds of support.

Now that you know what a Unity Breakfast is, I have to laugh when I think about going to mine. In fact, it became one of my favorite election stories. The Unity Breakfast in Illinois is a giant event held at a hotel in Chicago the morning after the election. It's meant to put the party back together, congratulate the losers for their hard work, and then, as a group, get behind the winning candidates with an eye on winning the general election.

Candidates need to sign up for the breakfast long before election day, when they're all sure they're going to be the winner! In fact, you think thoughts like "That will be my first event as "Congresswoman-elect." Throughout the primary campaign, as I said, people ask candidates if they will promise to throw all of their support toward "the other guy" if he/

she wins. I had stated many times that I would support whoever won, so I needed to go.

I think I cried all the way downtown. At one point, I made a wrong turn on State Street—one of Chicago's busiest—and was pulled over by a Chicago cop. He took my license and went back to his car to fill out the paperwork. I must have looked pathetic because when he returned to hand me the ticket, he asked if I was alright. I said I'd just lost my race for Congress. Suddenly this big tough cop got a funny look on his face and tore up the ticket, saying "Ahhh jeez, never mind this, just be more careful." I remember thinking "I didn't know they could tear up a ticket after they had written it—I must look like hell!"

It was hard, but I went to the breakfast, congratulated the winners, and saw my grief reflected in the faces of the others who didn't win either. I respected the ones who still showed up, and was surprised by some who not only didn't show up, but also later wrote off their campaign debt. After the election is over, you need to dismantle the organization that has grown to support you, and settle all outstanding debts. I was amazed that some candidates would ignore the debt as if the campaign were a different entity not attached in any way to their character.

Because of that experience, I pay attention to the actions of those who lost their race.. One remarkable example is Hillary Clinton on the day of Donald Trump's Inauguration. Like her or hate her, you have to say that her behavior at the Inauguration was extraordinary. She showed up and was gracious throughout the day. That had to be incredibly hard on many levels; but on that day she set an example that all women can emulate.

CHAPTER 15

Show the Office Due Respect & It Respects You Back

"The days you work are the best days."

Georgia O'Keefe

Running for office and winning, however, is a thrill. There is no way to adequately convey the pride, the joy, the anticipation and the excitement that you feel on winning your first race, unless it would be in moving into the physical office that will be yours. At that point, it is so real you no longer speak in "if" and "when."

Sitting behind the desk that represents your position is an awesome thing. It should inspire you just to be there. I'll tell you something Liz once told me that I know to be true from my own experience as well. She said that many years ago when she was just starting out as a "real" writer, she attended a writer's workshop at Ragdale, an artist's colony in Lake Forest, Illinois.

The dozen writers in attendance at this workshop each week gathered round the dining room table to work, critique, and learn. One of the writers, who also happened to work in the office at Ragdale, casually mentioned one night that the table they were sitting around was previously owned by the wonderful writer and poet, Carl Sandburg. You could have heard a pin drop. The room went from quiet chatter to total silence, and they all just looked at this huge table and all it had seen as it hosted Sandburg while he worked.

All kinds of things ran through their minds – did he eat there when he worked? Is he the one who forgot to use a coaster under his glass and made the water mark? Did he write the poem about Chicago's big shoulders while sitting there, and did he watch fog through windows and doors as he talked about its coming in on cat's feet? We'll never know. But a funny thing happened. Because they respected the "office" where they now sat to such a high degree, it raised the bar for their writing. They *all* became better writers; borrowing from the energy of the table and feeling that if "he" could sit there and write great things, so could they. And they did.

Something happens to us all when we are in the physical presence or the environment of something that's important to us. It's not about us, it's about the office. And that's another lesson we learn.

Speaking of lessons, we wonder what Sandburg would think of newspapers today. In his day they were, for the most part, bastions of truthfulness, held to high standards of factual research vs. today's sometimes "opinion-based" news. We might draw a parallel to them and Sandburg's table in that they represented a lot of searching, digging, laborious work that was done by writers and reporters in search of cold hard facts. "Just" the facts. Editorializing was left to the editors' pieces on the op-ed pages. Or to the "just plain folks" writing in to the editor who were not held to the same high standards as were the reporters.

Before Cable TV, the same was true for television newscasters as well. They stuck to "just the facts." Part of that may have been due to the half-hour news format that existed then versus today's twenty-four-hour news cycle. Twenty-four hours is a lot of time to fill with "just the facts." As more and more stations adopted that format, opinion began to creep in alongside actual news. There is nothing that is such a bane to television (or radio) as "dead air" when nobody is speaking and nothing is happening. It *must* be filled. It seemed natural for the newscasters to do some ad-libbing or improvising to fill that space.

It was a radical change from the time when Walter Cronkite, the evening anchor for CBS News, was voted the "most trusted man in America." If Walter said it, you could take it to the bank. The one and only time he showed emotion that betrayed his personal feelings was when he took off his glasses, cleared his throat, and somberly announced that he had gotten official word that President John F. Kennedy was now dead. And even then, he stuck to "just the facts," repeating them for emphasis, but never veering away from them.

Like so many things we have accepted in our culture today, are we accepting too little from our reporters, from our papers and from other news outlets? Since when has opinion replaced fact? "Just the facts" has been replaced with "Here's what I think," and "It seems to me." Not so good, in our opinion. Did you catch that? That last statement is our opinion, which is arguable, versus a newspaper clipping, which should be both factual and source based. We have in some ways regressed to where we were in colonial days before there were any accepted rules or guidelines for newspapers. We would like to see a return to opinions being labeled as such, and facts having proven-credible sources as their basis.

We *need* a credible source for the truth (good, bad, and ugly) and that truth should be the news. We, as readers, also need to take some responsibility and return to the practice of reading and then delving into further detail ourselves. That's really the only reliable way to develop an opinion which is credibly our own. Ask yourself, do I look for information to help me understand all sides of an issue—or do I, even subconsciously, seek out opinions which support my own? And while you're doing that also ask if when discussing issues do I listen to learn or do I listen only to rebut and hit someone over the head with my own opinion?

Here are several short examples from a small-town Mayor that show the need to focus on and the results from focusing on respect for those who disagree.

"As Mayor, I had to make sure this focus prevailed in our own community if I wanted nonpartisanship to be one of the major hallmarks of my administration. I made it a point *not* to identify board members as Democrat or Republican, and feel that may be part of the reason we accomplished so much economic growth in the middle of a recession.

"I think the key to making sure no-one is ever ostracized for a dissenting opinion is to keep discussions issue-oriented. Let me say that again: they were issue-oriented. *It should never be about you, or the members of your team.*

"But since we live in a world that *is not* ideal, the leader must find ways to tame huge and potentially destructive arguments into reasonable give-and-take discussions. That is a leader's job, from the smallest local office to the ultimate one in the White House.

"As a woman, you have probably learned techniques for doing just that by helping keep family arguments under control as they arise, and then escalate. Think about Thanksgiving...Christmas...every day. You've been there and done that already.

"Staying focused on issues versus people was one challenge; but I also found that separating people's political leanings and their friendship with me was one as well. Sometimes it was disappointing, but in all fairness, important to do. One example happened during my race for Congress. I ran as a Republican against the incumbent Democrat. One day I received a call from a friend who was also a neighbor, and who had been a great help in my campaign for mayor. She was a frequent volunteer; a concerned individual who was very active in our community; and a generally all-around good person.

"She called to tell me that, unfortunately, she couldn't vote for me. It was clear that this was a hard call for her to make, but she had the core values and principles that made her pick up the phone and do it. She told me that both she and her husband were strong Democrats, had helped the incumbent get elected in the first place, and had supported her ever since. With obvious emotion, she said she hoped it wouldn't negatively affect our friendship. It was one of the first times I was in that type of situation, but it wouldn't be the last. Maintaining friendships while on different sides politically was a good lesson to learn, and it served me well.

"I bring up this story because it illustrates how women are especially good at seeing the many "layers" of a situation and are now even recognized or noted for it. But realizing we see the big picture was the lesson that for me drove home the need to let others have their opinions. They are part of the picture too. *You still have common ground somewhere with them, and if you genuinely respect them as people, or at least respect the offices they hold, you will find it.*"

There is simply no room for pettiness in a small town, and ironically, that is often where you find it most. Senator Orrin Hatch of Utah wrote a recent op-ed article [36] addressing just this point, and stressing that if we all return to civility, politics can't help but do the same. One can only hope.

---

36   Senator Orrin Hatch, *I Am Re-Committing to Civility.* Time Ideas, Politics. June 28, 2017. http://time.com/4835019/orrin-hatch-civility-politics/ Accessed June 20, 2018.

CHAPTER 16

How Being In Office Works

*"I don't know that there are any shortcuts
to doing a good job."*

Justice Sandra Day O'Connor

We mentioned that the mayor's office, which usually also entails interacting with some form of town council, is a microcosm of our greater government. Indeed, it mirrors both the state level with its speaker, house, senate, and committees, as well as the United States Congress, which is of the same structure, simply larger in size. We gave the previous personal examples of ensuring issue-oriented discussions and respect for individuals because that is more important than ever, the higher you go in government. The stakes will be higher and the results more far reaching.

All levels must deal with individual member's peccadillos, as well as with committees vying for limited funds, large corporations vying with smaller interests, rural interests vying with city-based ones, etc. So many of the experiences you encounter either in campaigning or in holding office will ultimately be of the same type, just larger in scale the higher you climb.

The fact that the executive seat is not supposed to have a vote is another reminder that the mayor, governor, or president's job is to respectfully facilitate consensus among opposing philosophies. Maria notes she didn't think much about this needed skillset before she ran for office. But once installed, she realized facilitating respectful negotiation was one of her strengths. Together, from small towns to big cities, we can change the tone and quality of national debate if we commit to the idea of respecting a difference of opinion, and the opposing philosophy that generates it. Demonizing the other side of the political aisle is both counterproductive and degrading to our society as a whole.

While the circumstances may change over the years, the principles don't. This free exchange of ideas is what makes us an exceptional nation. It is remarkable to note that we were the first (and we believe the only) country in the world that is founded on ideals—freedom of speech, freedom of religion, freedom to assemble, among others—rather than on geography. We are the United States of America because our Founding Fathers reached consensus of their own on the principles that would guide us. Individual freedom was indeed one of those principles; but they recognized that individual responsibility to protect the country—and thus the ideals which defined it—went hand in hand with such freedom.

As Americans, we are encouraged to have our opinions. We feel free to agree or disagree without fear of retaliation. That means there is an unspoken expectation that we will, in turn, respect that freedom for others to do the same—recognizing that there is nothing inherently evil in having a philosophy different from someone else's—understanding that a different philosophy manifests itself in a different opinion.

We fear, sadly, however, that partisan polarization is now threatening that necessary process of respectful discussion to reach agreement. No one person or party has all the answers. The founding fathers knew the real solution is always somewhere in the middle. The words "by the people, for the people" take on a deeper meaning when you think carefully about this.

We need to be able to discuss our own opinion without concern that we will be ostracized. This is an important tenet of our great republic, and we should not let it become imperiled. Without such a commitment, there can be a portal for hate to enter. This is another good example of why we recommend working your way up and through the political system. By the time you run for President, the public has a demonstrated record of the needed skillsets you possess!

Maria points out it was enormously gratifying to work through some of the issues that plagued the village for years and to see growing consensus. Let her give you a couple examples of "small town" issues, and the various roles that respect must play in moving toward solutions. These examples are for "flavor" in communicating the politics of a small town, and we think they achieve that objective. Again, these are her own words.

At the Helm

My mayoral community was Long Grove, Illinois. It was and is a community with a very small staff and a government that depends on higher than average volunteer involvement. We also don't collect a village property tax; the village is funded by sales tax revenue and building permit fees. The zoning is based on an appreciation for open space and preservation of natural resources and landscape, traceable no doubt to the fact that originally these were small houses on large properties and the residents could be categorized as "sturdy folks." They didn't want the village to provide services that they could provide for themselves.

For example, they opted out of Lake Michigan Water for their water supply, choosing instead for all homes and businesses to be on wells and rely on septic systems instead of sewers. In addition, each property owner had to dedicate the lowland, or hydric soil areas, on his or her property to the village. I learned the importance of having this mandate while watching other communities without it deal with the resulting flooding and all its problems.

The hydric soils are the natural water retention ponds. When you disregard that fact, and build structures where these soils are, the water has no place to go. I frankly didn't really believe at first that wetlands could soak up such an incredible amount of water. I was placed on the Storm Water Management Board early on, however, and learned how incredibly important they are. Soon I began to act like an evangelist for the importance of wetlands!

A mayor can learn things like that which are wonderfully useful and forward thinking, while at the same time, other experiences can be downright weird. Keep in mind that I became mayor fifty years *after* the Village was incorporated. By that time, many of the new residents were building more affluent homes with higher taxes. As a result, our county taxes were high enough that unless Long Grove residents really scrutinized their tax bill, they assumed that property taxes were included in that amount. That led them to also assume that we therefore had the same services and staff as most other affluent villages in the area, and that those services basically covered anything they would need.

For example, one day I got a call from the Village Hall saying that a resident had called, demanding that a dead animal be picked up from his yard IMMEDIATELY. Even though hunting is not allowed, someone had evidently shot a deer in the nearby forest preserve and the wounded animal then wandered over to this guy's yard, where it soon died—directly under his kids' jungle gym.

That, for his children to find, would have been disturbing enough, but to add insult to injury, a coyote or some other animal ate the hind end of the deer in the middle of the night—you can't make this stuff up—leaving a picture worthy of a bad horror movie that greeted his family when they woke. His kids were understandably upset, if not traumatized, and of course it manifested itself as sheer chaos and a vale of tears as they were trying to get off to school.

The guy himself was hopping mad because "they" (Village Hall) told him that they would contact the county to have *its* (the county's) animal control division come pick it up. But he was also cautioned that being Monday morning, it might be a while. I decided to talk to him by phone and then stop by his house. Instinctively, I felt face-to-face would be best in this situation, although I wasn't particularly a fan of being shown the dead and ravaged deer.

I learned another lesson that day: people want to be heard. Talking with him face-to-face I could explain calmly that although I agreed it was a gruesome sight, the village neither owned the truck nor employed the staff to pick up a dead deer. I could also then assure him that, given the circumstances, we would press the county to make *his* pickup a priority. He was good with that and I took a second lesson to heart: trust your instincts; they will serve you well!

Although I believe in fiscal conservancy (taxes should only be for the essential functions of the government) the decision to not collect a Village property tax was shortsighted, to say the least. The problem was they then had no method to collect funds to maintain roads, bridges, and other necessary infrastructure. And they definitely had no animal pickup service.

Yet another lesson, and this is an important one, is that knowing the history of a situation and of your community itself is vital. If one side knew WHY the other side was upset, or WHY an issue was important to them, the two sides could resolve the conflict more quickly. It also then helps avoid poor decisions in the future.

Another time, early in my first term, the village manager showed me an email he had received from a resident saying that he couldn't believe we had this "Mexican mayor, Rodriguez," asking "...*is he even legal?*" Village manager Dave Lothspeich decided to reply to the man directly, stating that the new village mayor was not only *not* Mexican, (I'm Irish, married to a Cuban) but neither was she a man. I always wondered which bothered that emailer more—that I could have been Mexican or that I was a woman.

So, brace yourself for meeting all kinds of people with all kinds of situations and all kinds of outlooks toward both you and your office. Stay the course, remain humble, and do as First Lady Michelle Obama often advised, saying "When they go low, we go high." The high road does the trick every time, and all those different personalities I encountered added to the character of the Village and to my experience at the helm.

Not Alone

And when you are at the helm, you will find that not only will you be working with your village residents, but you will be reaching out to other "ships" as well. I truly enjoyed coordinating and interacting with other governmental bodies. I remember one time the elementary school asked for a small grant to establish a weather station there. The students came to the meeting and it was amazing to watch these third- or fourth-graders make the pitch. There were also countless scout groups and other civic-minded groups that added richness to the job.

A couple of times, I was asked to allow a child to be "Mayor for a Day," the chance for which was raffled off at different fundraisers. That was a remarkable experience as well. The chance to honor the older individuals in office long before I served is another fond memory. They had been so generous with their time and energy, building a village that was a source of both pride and joy.

I can tell you with certainty that government, at any level, is a ready platform for the best of the human condition to reveal itself. Of course, sometimes the human condition reveals itself as mischievous. For instance, I naturally promoted the village during all the summer festivals, and thoroughly enjoyed doing so—most of the time. It was great fun to support the merchants in whatever way they asked. The only time I wish I had said no, was for a pie eating contest at the Strawberry Festival. There is no graceful way to eat a strawberry pie with your hands tied behind your back, all the while knowing the picture will be in tomorrow's paper.

Long Grove was the definition of small government. I have included the things I have here to give you not only "flavor," but also a real taste of all that small-town government entails, both amusing and not so amusing. Some days felt like a Mayberry episode, to be sure; but all in all, the job was incredibly rewarding on multiple levels. But there were days that hit you with some real surprises.

Unintended Consequences

Taxes, or the lack thereof, aren't the only things that produce unintended consequences. They come from other areas as well, and they are just that—unintended. So, the better you get at anticipating every contingency you can think of and planning for it when you legislate, the better off you will be. People assume that their elected officials will automatically exercise that type of foresight.

For example, while I was in office two things happened simultaneously. First, the cost of petroleum hit an all-time high which *doubled* the cost of asphalt, since it contains a lot of petroleum. And second, the great recession hit. Builders were going out of business, leaving half-built properties, and of course not paying the permit fees that had been projected in our budget. The village had reserves, but we had moved investments over to Treasury Bills which yielded approximately one-half of one percent at that time. As a result, we had no way of finding revenue to do even the most modest maintenance. It was a wild time, to say the least. Projects were put on hold by every village department, and we all prepared for the grousing that inevitably followed.

As you have probably already figured out, some of the ideas espoused by the early farmers who settled here were well-intentioned but carried consequences. At the time of the original establishment of the village, fifty years before it was incorporated, it had one mile of public road, a one-room schoolhouse, and a general store. Requiring everyone to be on a private well and septic system seemed like a good idea back then. Not only did it support the necessity of everyone's lot being a large one to accommodate the septic field, it also meant, therefore, that the density would remain as originally visualized. In addition, it meant no need for supporting a public works department, but the unintended consequence was that it also meant no available services of a public works department to pick up dead deer from private property, etc.

It also didn't account for the fact that other towns were establishing themselves at the same time, creating a race that included Long Grove to see who could annex the most properties contiguous to their borders. The unintended consequence there was that coming along with all the newly annexed subdivisions were added public roads and the need for more services in general.

In about 1978, Long Grove built a large and relatively dense subdivision with a golf course in the middle. It was a new idea for a "planned unit development." Instead of demanding that *all homes* have from one to three acres of land, they used the "open space" of the golf course as part of the formula so that they could put the houses closer together. They also put in public roads. These were the last public roads built in the village. The unintended consequence here was that the village now had *thirty-eight miles of public roads*, and maintenance was going to be a huge issue. Eventually you would have to repair or replace, and Long Grove had neither tax money nor staff to do so.

The decision made to not collect property taxes was made with forethought, not just willy-nilly. It was based on the vision back then that the village's needed revenue would be funded by building-permit fees and sales-tax revenue from the shops of the little town fast becoming an antique market mecca.

Avoiding unintended consequences is at the crux of our governmental process. If you circumvent the process, foregoing discovery and debate, you end up with poorly written legislation, far-reaching commitments, and a whole boatload of unintended consequences.

Following the process, however, sometimes forces the government to move so slowly it's frustrating. But it *is* necessary. When you're debating the details of new laws, you have to be less independent minded and more big-picture oriented. And as we said, women are good at that! Big-picture thinking requires you to ask and answer, "What is the best decision for the most people with the least fallout for the rest?" The answer to that is rarely simple. Multiple questions must be raised and satisfactory answers given.

Sometimes you need engineering input, for instance. You must have everything done correctly and to code so that you can be confident in its sustainability. Sustainability is an overused buzzword today, but the point remains valid. You need laws in place that have a long-term benefit. Everything the government sponsors, whether it be laws or physical structures like roads and bridges, has to be able to stand the test of time.

Process also includes having legal as well as engineering input to make sure the laws include ways to provide enforcement, preventing residents from jury-rigging something to "make do" or completely neglecting to comply with a law. In addition, there must also be redress for one resident's causing harm to another through personal negligence. In other words, there's a lot to think about behind every law that goes forward. The leader is in charge of making sure all these bases are covered, if not personally, at least by those lawfully delegated. Fortunately, women are quite used to covering all the bases.

And you know what? Female leaders take great pride in doing just that. Susan Garrett, for instance, whom was mentioned earlier seemed to embody most women political leaders' outlook when she said, "I'm a strong believer in that when something's wrong, you must stand up and try to correct it."

She was, in fact, often known for leading the charge; which, she points out, is how she got into politics in the first place. When her party "came calling" it was because members said her name always came up as someone who was not afraid to put herself out there, nor to have her name attached to something she believed needed to be raised as an issue and widely discussed. And like most women politicians, she also trusted her instincts to tell her when her voice would be effective and when it wouldn't, letting instincts guide her as to when to bring up issues, when to run, what office to seek, and when to retire or move on. And women usually get that just right.

CHAPTER 17

From the Ridiculous To the Sublime

"Never go to a doctor whose office plants have died."

Erma Bombeck

Most days in politics are filled with meetings. As in most leadership positions, any mayor learns the value of delegating responsibility to others. Delegation enables a group to accomplish what a single individual never could on his or her own. I was lucky to have a village manager who with his staff eased the learning curve. I am certain that I would not have been able to accomplish what I did without their help.

Just to include soup to nuts, let me assure you that there comes a day when you realize that you are going to get blamed for everything bad that happens under your administration and sometimes even criticized for the good things that you do. That is an important realization because it helps you to rise above criticism. Most people will, in fact, be on your side—even if you are going to vote against what they want—if they feel they were listened to and heard, *and they hear* the well-thought-out reasons for the action you take.

And here's a good piece of advice. In politics, people continually say things to you and want an immediate response. But you will likely need more information, including some history. The word "Hmmmm" can be a go-to response in cases like that. It buys you time, and gets the other person to realize you need to know more. And by the way, it works on all age groups!

Looking Back

Looking back on my political career, did I accomplish what I wanted to? I would say that I did, though there was the usual frustration of not having finished absolutely *everything* needing to be done. Eight years sounds like such a long time to have been mayor; but you have to look at where things were when you started and respect the fact that the government moves slowly if it includes all the debate, inclusion, and discovery that I touted so highly. And that's a good thing.

Businesses in many small towns across America were suffering because of the recession, big box stores, and the Internet. So, restoring a little downtown like ours became a real challenge. Getting the long-term plan and its funding mechanisms in place was one of my main concentrations during my tenure as mayor, and I feel, one of my greatest accomplishments. There is always still "more" to do, of course, and it takes a lot of individuals putting in a lot of hours. You always have to work around the economic surprises. But I feel that I laid the groundwork and started the process. Complete revitalization of the historic business district is no longer an "if," but is now a "when." The time it takes to finish the job will depend on a variety of factors, not the least of which is the ability of future board members and other town officials to not only work well together, but also to work well with the residents.

In a small town, people are passionate about their neighborhood, and if something is happening that they don't like, they show up at a Board meeting. When they showed up, we used to joke that we could envision the pitchforks and torches of a former time. It was usually NIMBY (Not In My Backyard) issues, like cell towers in the yard across the street, that brought out the angry crowds. But, in all honesty, you could expect anything!

That's what happened with the infamous sewer project. People who didn't like our choice showed up repeatedly at meetings, debating the points over and over, even once the better choice became clear. But to them, at that time this was the most important matter and most critical decision in the world. And as their elected officials, we had the obligation to hear them out, at least until nothing else was left to say! Here's what happened.

One of the first things I had to deal with was the installation of a big box home improvement store that had been approved just before I took office. Part of the development required that a sewer had to be put in. So, I learned more about sewers than I ever dreamed I would. I discovered there are two types, each with its own set of pros and cons, and it fell to the Board to determine which would be best—meaning of course, the best for everyone, or at least for the majority.

The first type, the gravitational sewer, requires a "lift station" that's monitored by the county through those green metal boxes (they house the controls) that you see here and there as you drive around a town. This is necessary because the waste disposal relies on gravity for the pull into the sewer. Then the mechanism must be "lifted up" and pitched to the correct angle again. The controls housed in the "green box" deal with all that.

The undeniable pro to the lift type is that it offers access to *all* the homes that are near it. This was of great importance to Long Grove, because it provided a viable one-time option for those residents whose septic fields were older, failing, and needed to be replaced. The sewer would be a one-time expense, and the best location for the lift station green box was one that was actually only visible to a few homes.

The alternative that was not chosen was a "forced main" sewer. That type can only be tapped into *at certain points* along its path. Because it is literally a "million dollar a mile" project, houses that were too far from others would be left out for budgetary reasons. Economically it would simply not be feasible to run more "million-dollar" miles of additional pipe off the main path of the sewer. This would leave many of the "distant" residents out of luck.

So, our job was to see the big picture of what would be the best solution for the most residents; and that was indeed the gravitational-feed sewer system. Ten years later, it has become a non-issue. Shrubbery mostly conceals the lift station now, proving that sometimes you simply must stand your ground, knowing that what you are doing is truly for the good and the betterment of your community.

That still, however, didn't quite prepare me for the disgruntled residents coming to the meetings to complain about the duration, extent, and inconvenience of the project.

But you have to let things like that roll off you back. Chances are you probably won't have to deal with something of that magnitude right after being elected. If you do, however, remember that people have emotional responses, and you, as the leader, need to keep your own in check in order to create balance and move the project ahead.

While we're talking about emotions, reactions, and all the feelings we have to deal with both while running and in the job, let's touch on how they differ in major ways from campaign to campaign, and how that teaches us incredibly important things about ourselves. I've talked about running for Congress during my first term as mayor, then going back to the mayoral post, but most recently, I was approached by two gubernatorial candidates to run with them as their choice for Lieutenant Governor.

I said yes to State Senator Bill Brady whom I admired both then and now. We shared the same position on most issues, and I felt he had both the experience and established relationships to be an effective governor. I hoped to build on his previous political successes, and, since his campaign had already started, help give his candidacy a final push. We did not win, but the lessons learned were invaluable, and the differences from my other campaigns are worth highlighting here.

Throughout the book, we have noted that general campaign practices are in place for any campaign. However, there are subtle differences that are good to know when deciding if a particular office would be for you. Different offices require different personal strengths. For example, local office means you're talking about neighborhood issues, and you will physically interact with constituents daily at the grocery store or gas station as well as at board meetings. Serving in Congress requires high-level decisions that impact the entire country, and sometimes even the world.

Yet a Congressional District is a relatively reasonable size, meaning you still can have a personal relationship with constituents.

Campaigning for Governor is a different animal altogether. A gubernatorial campaign is in many ways a microcosm of a presidential campaign, because you are usually campaigning in widely diverse regions, even though it is only statewide. In the same way that pressing issues are different for people in Texas compared to people in New York, Chicagoans, for example, may prioritize problems differently than residents in southern Illinois, as we talked about earlier. Since the sheer logistics of large states can be as daunting as in a nationwide campaign, you need many volunteers to tailor the message and events around the state to the needs of that specific region.

Another similarity to a presidential campaign is that in gubernatorial races in some states, candidates run as a dual ticket. Just as a presidential candidate chooses a running mate to run for Vice President, a candidate for Governor in such states has to select a running mate to run on the ticket for Lieutenant Governor. Illinois is such a state, which is why I was asked to run with Senator Bill Brady.

I joined his campaign, already in progress, and as are most, it was a whirlwind from the start. I met some extraordinary people! I also have to confess to becoming acutely aware of my "modest" control needs. (Liz made me swear to put the word "modest" in quotes.) In my past campaigns, I was solely responsible for the campaign decisions, and their outcome as well, whether positive or negative. This time, I was running as the "wingman," and although Brady was always respectful of my suggestions, it was *his* campaign for Governor and I was in a supporting role, a very different experience for me. I am pointing out the difference in the campaign "experience" because some people are, frankly, not suited to be "vice-" anything.

I stress this because often a candidate does not realize how much of a secondary role he or she is accepting, and it comes as a bit of a shock to subordinate your own opinions in favor of the candidate's or the platform's. We do not want you to have to face any surprises along the way that we can call to your attention ahead of time. So, keep in mind that any position such as Lt. Governor, Vice-President, or Associate Director, by definition, will place you in more of an "advocate" or "supporting" role than you may wish. What is *your* level of need to control your everyday agenda? It's something to think about!

I will tell you this, however: no matter the differences from one office to another, win or lose it's a wonderful experience to know you have added something of worth to a campaign. In that one, I brought my northern Illinois connections, networks, and constituents to complement his from further south. I also brought a woman's perspective to all the issues. We remain friends to this day, and in fact occasionally work together on Illinois issues. (Most recently, Senator Brady appointed me to the Illinois Senate Task Force on Sexual Discrimination & Harassment Awareness & Prevention. We're both anxious to see progress in this area.)

Having experienced such a range of campaigns, I've seen that there are always surprises. The truth is, everyone gets into the race because he or she thinks they can win. And sometimes the longshot wins the race. So never think your opponent can't win; or even worse, sit back and think the race is in the bag. Political highways are littered with folks who did that. Don't be one of them. Keep centered on doing useful work that's going to get you your needed votes and cover the unexpected shifts in voting patterns. There is nothing wrong with having a few extra votes in your corner!

This "work till the end of the race" mentality is also important because in any election you have volunteers who are working very hard day and night. You certainly want to be setting an exemplary and productive pace, or they could easily feel resentful and lose their motivation. After all, they're not even getting paid for working so hard (multiple pizzas do not count.)

Appointed Positions

At every level of the government, there are not just elected positions, but appointed positions as well. They run the gamut from planning commission or architectural board at the local level to working as a volunteer staff member for higher-level elected officials. In fact, some people use appointed positions as stepping stones to running for elected office. The degree of your personal involvement will vary, and again is totally up to you. Trust your instincts about which is the right starting place for you. Chances are pretty good you are right.

An Order of Grit To Go

If your mother, like Liz's, was from an earlier time where the option to run for office was not easily available to women, I'm sure you saw her step up in other ways. In her seventies, in the cold and dreary winter weather of Chicago in 1968, Liz's mom wore a "sandwich board" sign and marched up and down the streets of her small town in her winter coat, red rubber boots and jaunty beret to support her candidate, her hand-drawn back and front signs clearly spelling out why. People half her age didn't do half as much! So, the lessons learned from observing mothers have always been there, just not always in the form of observing them as candidates! They worked with what they had. What you have as a woman—mentally, physically, and experientially is enough to make a difference.

Let's continue to talk about making a difference. Once you realize how skilled you are, your confidence level rises and it shows in all sorts of ways. Amazingly, you find yourself making a difference at the oddest times and places. Maybe it's time to finally tell Liz's California story.

In the 1990's, while living in Chicago, Liz handled the West Coast as a sales territory and sold advertising space in trade journals. To keep expenses under control, she would often spend two weeks at a time out there; and to make it feel less lonely on the road, she had certain habits. Always stay in the same hotel, so they know you. Always put your clothes in the same drawers in each hotel room so it seems more like your setup at home. Find a good place for lunch and be a regular there as much as schedule permits.

One day while Liz was having lunch at her chosen spot, the waitress saw her intently poring over a media kit and commented that one day she would like to have a job that looked that interesting. Liz looked up and smiled and the waitress continued, "I'd like to get a really good paying job and move into a better place with my daughter and have a bit nicer life for both of us."

Liz put down her pen and said to her, "Well don't just tell *me* about it, then. Make it happen! Get a pencil and a piece of paper and figure out how much it would cost you to live for three months without income while you looked for a job. Then figure how long it would take you to save that amount. Start saving up today. Work some extra hours. When you *know* you can get by for three months, quit the waitressing and go find what you really want."

She pulled out one of her business cards and handed it to her. "You can do this. Here's my card if you ever need some help trying to get into publishing or ad sales." The waitress thanked her, and that was that.

Time passed, and Liz had totally forgotten the incident. But two or three years later she got a note from "the waitress" addressed to Liz at her business. It said:

"Dear Ms. Richards,

You might not remember me, but I used to be your waitress in

Fountain Valley at lunchtime. I just wanted to write and thank you for how you've changed my life. I did what you said and saved up the money so I could look for the right job and not have to worry about paying bills while I did. It was incredible...I found the perfect thing in two months of looking, which meant I had the rest of the money left over and could soon move into a better place.

I am currently in management training for the company, and have great hopes for my future. Thanks so much for your help. God bless you.

Sincerely, "

Liz was surprised to hear she had that much influence. She, like so many women, had been exercising leadership without even thinking about it. How about you? If you think back, can you recall being an influence on someone?

CHAPTER 18

Theories Worth Thinking About

"And the trouble is, if you don't risk anything,
you risk even more."

Erica Jong

One thing, however, that still seems to hold women back (at least a good number of them) is that unlike men, they often feel they must be ready at every level to apply for a job. We mentioned earlier that 80% of men think nothing of applying for jobs for which they don't fully qualify. Muscling and charming their way in, they are confident that whatever skill they lack can be quickly learned.

We also pointed out that women are typically just the opposite. Up to 80% of them would NOT apply for a job where they do not meet all the stated requirements. This, hopefully will soon change as more and more women realize they are indeed qualified, and can learn new skills as needed. After all, they often earn the equivalent of an MBA from daily experience in their own backyard!

There is another theory (in addition to the one about smart girls' attitudes about themselves changing in middle school) that girls as young as six or seven begin to think of themselves as less capable both intellectually and athletically. This theory, though we are unsure of its origin, is the stated motivation behind the Proctor & Gamble *Run Like a Girl*™ campaign, where running like a girl is initially considered undesirable to the girls, and even seen as a handicap. We ask you to consider if our culture is indeed abetting this attitude, and if so, we need to change that. That's what P&G does in its ads, making running like a girl be something to be proud of, symbolizing both strength and ability. Maybe you have an idea how to support that change. If so, don't be shy. Email us at mr4159@gmail.com and lizthetraveler@gmail.com.

Another campaign with which we are probably all familiar is Dove™ Soap's *Real Beauty* campaign. Kudos to both companies for each tackling something about self-image that has been reinforced for years, and known to hold women back. Things like this are finally beginning to get the notice they deserve.

In a recent Associated Press article http://www.usnews.com/news/politics/articles/2017-01-27/little-girls-doubt-that-women-can-be-brilliant-study-shows?src=usn_fb2017 Rebecca S. Bigler, professor of psychology at the University of Texas at Austin, is referenced as suggesting that "Stereotypes develop in early elementary school when students are exposed to famous scientists, composers and writers, the 'geniuses' of history who are overwhelmingly men." [37] Bigler said it is important to combine that knowledge with information on gender discrimination.

In addition to that suggestion from Bigler, we think it is incumbent upon all of us women to have ready examples of female contributors who did exist but were not always promoted. Examples would be Madame Curie, the NASA space "computers" about whom a movie was recently made—math and logic geniuses, all. Women are functioning every day on a par with men in research labs and famous clinics as both researchers and practicing doctors.

And at last we have a fair share of women on the Supreme Court, with Elena Kagan, Sonia Sotomayor, and the irrepressible Ruth Bader Ginsberg. And we cannot forget The Honorable Sandra Day O'Connor who broke the glass ceiling in that venerable chamber, and remains a force to be reckoned with in retirement today.

---

37   Rebecca Bigler, Ph.D., University of Texas at Austin quoted by Maria Danalova in AP Article, Jan 26, 2017 about study published in journal, *Science*. http://www.usnews.com/news/politics/articles/2017-01-27/little-girls-doubt-that-women-can-be-brilliant-study-shows?src=usn_fb2017

Finally, another governmental glass ceiling was broken when Nancy Pelosi was named first female Speaker of the House, making her the highest level female politician in the land, and third in the succession line for the presidency of the United States. We're getting there, but as a culture we need to stress the long journey it has been, so girls feel proud to own and continue it. We're pleased to hear there is a huge surge in the number of women planning to run for office both in the midterm and the next general election. More signs yet there is a new movement afoot.

The Leader Is You

When a mother, or any woman, runs for office, it shows young girls in no uncertain terms that it's appropriate for a woman to be in high-level leadership positions. This is one good way to confront the old stereotype that's more impactful than telling young girls that there have been laws passed to help guard against discrimination. We need women of all ages! As you age, don't count yourself out. The wisdom you bring is VITALLY important to use now, and to share as a mentor.

It is also a way to genuinely make a difference. It's not just about protesting and/or participating in a march. Remember what we said: marching lets you make a statement, but getting elected lets you make laws. Women need to be a voice at the table. They need to be part of the solution, *and can be* by plugging in to their unique and natural strengths. If you think you're not smart enough, think again! You're smarter than you think, and are continually getting smarter, according to a study by the *Happiness Advantage* [38] project on how brain connectors increase when needed or tasked with new challenges.

Read a lot, and read quality. At least, make time for the magazines or newspapers you respect, and don't be shy about quoting them. As we said earlier, start the conversation. One way to start is to become a regular follower of the website for the movement Maria started called "The Leader Is You" at theleaderisyou.com. This book is part of the umbrella of facts,

---

38   Shawn Achor, *The Happiness Advantage*. 2010, Crown Business, New York, New York.

suggestions, and other important information housed there, even though the book does also have its own website, www.runjanerunbook.com.

But Wait, There's More

In the next (fourth) part of the book, you will find helpful resources and references for further reading, some in print and others in electronic format. You will also find lists of organizations and websites that are designed for helping women get elected. And don't forget, once you declare your intention to run, political organizations will jump at the chance to work with a solid candidate like you. The final item under Resources & References is the state-by-state (alpha order) list of state Boards of Election with contact information. Our acknowledgements are also in Part Four.

We thank you for reading this book. We thank you for caring enough to consider running or volunteering. And we thank you for being the type of strong confident woman determined to leave this country and this world a better place for having been in it. Feel free to contact either of us at any time to discuss politics. We'll never turn you down. Here are our emails again, so you don't have to double back to the previous section to find them: mr4159@gmail.com and lizthetraveler@gmail.com.

May God continue to bless this great country with powerful, inspiring, and talented women who *never* stop being involved! Let's move on to Part Four, where we hear some final thoughts from those currently contributing to our political landscape.

PART FOUR

CLOSING THOUGHTS & RESOURCES

CHAPTER 19

Political Sisters Weigh In: Musings on Political Life

It's amazing, but even though the women with whom we spoke are from different parties, come from different backgrounds, and are different ages, serving in different areas of the political spectrum, their musings, conclusions, regrets, or disappointments are remarkably similar. We found that Maria's experiences were indeed representative of so many others, that we did not feel the need to duplicate quotes or experiences.

Having said that, there was one experience that we didn't mention with the others that bears mentioning here. That is the way in which JoAnn DeRue Osmond of Northern Illinois got into politics. JoAnn was married to Illinois State Representative Tim Osmond, who died in office, while still quite young. JoAnn subsequently was appointed to fulfill her husband's term. She then went on to be elected six more times for a total of twelve-and-a-half years. She continued her husband's work, while starting and accomplishing her own, serving on various committees over the years. She told Liz:

"After my husband died, his seat in the statehouse was vacant. He had done so much good, for both the people and the party, that I was approached to run for his seat and carry on that work. I talked to my grown children, and then met with the party officials as a family. One of my kids asked, 'Is there any way she can screw this up?' When they replied, "No," almost in unison my kids said, 'Go for it, Mom.'

And I did. That was over twenty-some years ago. I've done my part—for my husband, and myself, and the people of 'our' district." [39]

JoAnn, like Sonny Bono's wife in California, had a sad and unusual start to her journey in politics by running for a seat previously held by her deceased husband. But each found that politics suited her, and would remain in it, contributing substantially every year that she did. We bring it up to show yet another strength of so many of the women we find in office, just as in the female trailblazers we listed earlier, and that is the ability to take a sadness and turn it into something productive, for both themselves and their country.

In researching this book, in addition to asking women what led them into politics, we asked what they found when they got there, what surprised them the most, angered them the most, and left them most dumbfounded. We asked about lessons learned, battles won and lost, opportunities missed or captured, and how politics had changed them. We heard about family, friendships, awe-inspiring moments, and heartbreaking times. They told us what they accomplished and what they still wish they might have. They, along with Maria, were totally honest.

They told us yes, there are things you will come across that you wish were different. You may, for instance, have to run against another fine and well-qualified woman whom you would otherwise support. You may sometimes see yourself as a "token" or a "tool" or a "target." It will cost money, time, and most of your energy. You may be blamed for things you didn't say or do. But guess what—*none* of these women said they were sorry that they had run or that they wished they hadn't.

Instead, they see themselves as trailblazers. They hold under ten percent of the governorships in this country. There are only (as of this writing) twenty-one of them out of the one-hundred current Senators. But they are smart, vocal, talented, compassionate, and flexible. And they persist. They could probably use the company of a few more like themselves. Why not you? After all, now you know how to get there. Run, Jane, run…we need you in office!

---

39   JoAnn Osmond, Interview with Liz Samuel Richards on March 7, 2017, Antioch, Illinois

Acknowledgements & Gratitude

To those of you who have read this book, we thank you! We hope it helped you see how you are well equipped for the political arena. Writing it has been exhilarating, sometimes exhausting, but always enlightening, especially for two women with such different backgrounds and party affiliations. Each of us has grown, developed an even higher tolerance for the opposing view, and coexisted with the other without coming to physical blows (although twice it was close.) We think the results were worth it, and hope you agree.

To the media, who thought enough of this project to help us get the word out through blogs, columns, interviews, and articles, we appreciate your gracious assistance in reaching our audience.

To those who helped us place and sell this book, we owe a thank-you as well. Please know how grateful we are for your help and support. Thank you for believing in our own belief in women everywhere.

To the women from the political arena who took time from their busy schedules to give us their thoughts, share their stories, and lend even greater credence to our project's final version, we are so grateful! A special shout-out to Christine Radogno, Susan Garrett, JoAnn Osmond, Kathy Ryg and Sheila Schultz for sitting down specifically for this book to offer perspective from both sides of the aisle. We are grateful for your time spent in office and hope this book not only recognizes your contributions, but also serves as inspiration for women across the country.

To all of our "first readers": Amy Richards, Val McVey, Karen Schmitt, Diane Dowd, Geraldine Rodriguez and Chris Geiselhart, thank you for your precious time and fresh eyes. We so value your input, concrete suggestions, and constructive criticisms. Whether correcting grammar, adding thoughts, telling stories, or questioning assumptions, you all helped make the book the best it could be.

For those additional friends who over the past year made themselves available as sounding boards, willing to step in at a moment's notice to help shape our message, thank you for listening endlessly and for your thoughtful questions. Nancy Scannell, Crystal Maleski, Jenn Marshall, Pam Thomson, Martha Blackburn, Krystyna Gluc, Roger Pauly, Frank D'Argento, Duana Welch, Jane Ellen Keroson, Andrea Roberts, Ron Friedman, and Darla Temple are but a few that come to mind. In the course of the year, others heard of this project and not only spurred us on but gave us insight. We thank you too.

And finally, no acknowledgement could be more heartfelt than the one going to each of our families for being there for us through the agony and ecstasy of birthing this work. We know that sometimes it was all that was on our minds, but at least you never said we were out of them!

Liz: For my daughter's love and ongoing support, even when everything but the book seemed to take second place during this crazy year, I am so grateful. Love you!

Maria: To my husband Ray, who has continually supported me, never once saying, "That's a crazy idea;" to my children for their thoughtful critique, valuable IT help and willingness to cheer every tiny victory; to my siblings and their spouses for not pretending they were out of earshot when I talked constantly about this book; and of course, to my wonderful mother, for her good counsel and lifelong positive attitude. All of you have helped to make my dream come true. Love you!

Resources & References

We hope that women from all occupations, parties, and stations in life will be reading this book. We therefore have tried to include a sampling of books, organizations, and online resources that will offer at least something for everyone to advance political savvy and help them or someone they support get elected.

Please do not consider its listing here to be an endorsement by either author of any resource shown. Nor does the lack of listing of any book, organization, or website in any way imply that it would not be worth your time to explore. It is up to you, the reader, to do the specific research needed to see which ones (if any) align with your personal and/or political beliefs or aspirations. We list them in no particular order, and hope you find them useful.

Books on Strong Women:

- *Still I Rise,* by Marlene Wagman-Geller
- *The Book of Awesome Women: Boundary Breakers, Freedom Fighters, Sheroes & Female Firsts* by Becca Anderson
- *Women In Science: 50 Fearless Pioneers Who Changed the World* by Rachel Ignotofsky
- *Liar, Temptress, Solder, Spy* by Karen Abbott
- *Twenty Years at Hull House* by Jane Addams

And for Your Children, Here Are Three Young Adult Books On Strong Women:

- *Rad Women Worldwide: Artists and Athletes, Pirates and Punks, and Other Revolutionaries Who Shaped History* by Kate Schatz (for grades 6-8)

- *Rad American Women A-Z: Rebels, Trailblazers and Visionaries Who Shaped our History...and Our Future* by Kate Schatz (for grades 5 and up)

- *Girls Can Do Anything: From Sports to Innovation, Art to Politics, Meet Over 200 Women Who Got There First* by Caitlin Doyle

Books That Provide Historical Political Background to Today:

- *Parlor Politics: In Which the Ladies of Washington Help Build a City and a Government* by Catherine Allgor

- *Ladies of Liberty: The Women Who Shaped Our Nation* by Cokie Roberts

- *The Sixties – Years of Hope Days of Rage* by Todd Gitlin

- *Remembering America* by Richard Goodwin

- *Legislative Women: Getting Elected, Getting Ahead* by Beth Reingold

- *Women At the Table* by Michaeline Della Fera

- *The Political Campaign Desk Reference: A Guide for Campaign Managers and Candidates* by Michael McNamara

- *Rules for Revolutionaries – How Big Organizing Can Change Everything* by Becky Bond and Zach Exley

- *Shattered – Inside the Doomed Campaign of Hillary Clinton* by Jonathan Allen and Amie Parnes

- *Patriotic Grace: What It Is, and Why We Need It Now* by Peggy Noonan

- *Quotable Women of the Twentieth Century,* Edited by Tracy Quinn

Books On Leadership:

- *The Courage To Take Command* by Colonel Jill Morgenthaler, U.S. Army (Ret.)

- *Daring Greatly* by Brene Brown

- *Presence: Bringing Your Boldest Self to Your Biggest Challenges* by Amy Cuddy

- *Lean In: Women, Work, and the Will To Lead* by Sheryl Sandberg

- *Leading Gracefully: A Woman's Guide to Confident, Authentic, & Effective Leadership* by Monique Svazlion Tallon

- *See You At the Top* by Zig Ziglar

- *The Happiness Advantage* by Shawn Acho

Papers & Studies on Civics:

- **http://www.civxsummit.org/documents/ v1/SummitWhitePaper.pdf**

  ☐ The Republic is (Still) at Risk—and Civics is Part of the Solution – briefing paper for the Democracy at a Crossroads National Summit in Washington D.C. by Peter Levine and Kei Kawashima-Ginsberg of the Jonathan M. Tisch College of Civic Life at Tufts University. September 21, 2017.

- **http://civicmission.s3.amazonaws.com/118/ f0/5/171/1/Guardian-of-Demcracy-report.pdf**

  ☐ Guardians of Democracy – report by the Mission of Schools outlining six proven practices of effective civics education, with recommendations for policy makers.

Organizations Providing Information & Support for Women Who Run for Office:

- **She Should Run** (sheshouldrun.org)
- **Winning for Women** (winningforwomen.com)
- **Emily's List** (emilyslist.org)
- **Susan B. Anthony List** (sba-list.org)
- **Vote Run Lead** (voterunlead.org)
- **Representation 2020** (representwomen.org)
- **SRBWI—Southern Rural Black Women's Initiative** (srbwi.org)
- **Higher Heights for America** (higherheightsforamerica.com)
- **Running Start** (runningstartonline.org)
- **Political Party** (politicalparty.org)
- **Women's Campaign School at Yale University** (wcsyale.org)
- **IGNITE** (ignitenational.org)

Beginning on the next page, you will find a list of all the Boards of Election for the United States, in alpha order. We hope you will use it to great advantage!

STATE	OFFICE	WEBSITE	TELEPHONE
Alabama	Elections Division, Office of the Secretary of State, Montgomery, AL	http://www.alabamavotes.gov/	800/274-8683 334/242-7210
Alaska	Division of Elections, Office of the Lieutenant Governor, Juneau, AK	http://www.elections.alaska.gov	907/465-4611
American Samoa	Election Office, Pago Pago, AS	http://americansamoaelectionoffice.org	684/699-3570
Arizona	Elections Division, Office of the Secretary of State, Phoenix, AZ	http://www.azsos.gov/elections	602/542-0681
Arkansas	Elections Division, Office of the Secretary of State, Little Rock, AR	http://www.sos.arkansas.gov/ elections/Pages/default.aspx	800/482-1127 501/682-5070
California	Elections Division, Office of the Secretary of State, Sacramento, CA	http://www.sos.ca.gov/elections	800/345-8683 916/657-2166
Colorado	Elections Division, Office of the Secretary of State, Denver, CO	http://www.sos.state. co.us/pubs/elections/main. html?menuheaders=4	303/894-2200

Connecticut	Legislation and Election Administration Division, Office of the Secretary of the State, Hartford, CT	http://www.sots.ct.gov/sots/cwp/view.asp?a=3172&q=525432	800/540-3764 860/509-6100
Delaware	Office of the State Election Commissioner, Dover, DE	http://elections.delaware.gov	302/739-4277
District of Columbia	Board of Elections, Washington, DC	http://www.dcboee.org	202/727-2525
Florida	Division of Elections, Office of the Secretary of State, Tallahassee, FL	http://dos.myflorida.com/elections/	850/245-6200
Georgia	Elections Division, Office of the Secretary of State, Atlanta, GA	http://sos.ga.gov	404/656-2871
Guam	Guam Election Commission, Hagatna, GU	http://gec.guam.gov	671/477-9791
Hawaii	Office of Elections, Honolulu, HI	http://elections.hawaii.gov/	800/442-8683 808/453-8683
Idaho	Elections Division, Office of the Secretary of State, Boise, ID	http://www.sos.idaho.gov/elect/eleindex.htm	208/334-2852

Illinois	Illinois State Board of Elections, Springfield, IL	http://www.elections.il.gov	217/782-4141
Indiana	Indiana Election Division, Office of the Secretary of State, Indianapolis, IN	http://www.in.gov/sos/elections	800/622-4941 317/232-3939
Iowa	Office of the Secretary of State, Des Moines, IA	http://sos.iowa.gov	888/767-8683 515/281-0145
Kansas	Elections Division, Office of the Secretary of State, Topeka, KS	http://www.sos.ks.gov	787/296-4561
Kentucky (Candidates on Ballot)	Office of the Secretary of State, Frankfort, KY	http://www.sos.ky.gov/elections/Pages/default.aspx	502/564-3490
Kentucky (Election Results)	State Board of Elections, Frankfort, KY	http://elect.ky.gov/Pages/default.aspx	502/573-7100
Louisiana	Elections Division, Office of the Secretary of State, Baton Rouge, LA	http://www.sos.la.gov/ElectionsAndVoting/Pages/default.aspx	225/922-0900
Maine	Bureau of Corporations, Elections and Commissions, Office of the Secretary of State, Augusta, ME	http://www.maine.gov/sos	207/624-7650

Maryland	State Board of Elections, Annapolis, MD	http://www.elections.maryland.gov	800/222-8683 410/269-2840
Massachusetts	Elections Division, Office of the Secretary of the Commonwealth, Boston, MA	http://www.sec.state.ma.us/ele/eleidx.htm	800/462-8683 617/727-2828
Michigan	Elections Bureau, Office of the Secretary of State, Lansing, MI	http://www.michigan.gov/sos/0,4670,7-127-1633---,00.html	517/373-2540
Minnesota	Elections Division, Office of the Secretary of State, St. Paul, MN	http://www.sos.state.mn.us/elections-voting/	877/600-8683 651/215-1440
Mississippi	Elections Division, Office of the Secretary of State, Jackson, MS	http://www.sos.ms.gov/Elections-Voting/Pages/default.aspx	800/829-6786 601/359-6360
Missouri	Office of the Secretary of State, Jefferson City, MO	http://www.sos.mo.gov/elections	800/669-8683 573/751-2301
Montana	Office of the Secretary of State, Helena, MT	http://www.sos.mt.gov/Elections/index.asp	888/884-8683 406/444-5376
Nebraska	Office of the Secretary of State, Lincoln, NE	http://www.sos.ne.gov	402/471-2555

Nevada	Office of the Secretary of State, Carson City, NV	http://www.nvsos.gov/index.aspx?page=3	800/450-8594 775/684-5705
New Hampshire	Office of the Secretary of State, Concord, NH	http://sos.nh.gov/Elections.aspx	603/271-3242
New Jersey	Division of Elections, Office of the Secretary of State, Trenton, NJ	http://www.state.nj.us/state/elections/index.html	609/292-3760
New Mexico	Office of the Secretary of State, Santa Fe, NM	http://www.sos.state.nm.us	800/477-3632 505/827-3600
New York	State Board of Elections, Albany, NY	http://www.elections.ny.gov	518/474-8100
North Carolina	State Board of Elections, Raleigh, NC	http://www.ncsbe.gov/ncsbe	866/522-4723 919/733-7173
North Dakota	Office of the Secretary of State, Bismarck, ND	http://sos.nd.gov/elections	800/352-0867 701/328-4146
Northern Mariana Islands	Commonwealth Election Commission, Saipan, MP	http://www.votecnmi.gov.mp	670/664-8683
Ohio	Elections Division, Office of the Secretary of State, Columbus, OH	http://www.sos.state.oh.us/SOS/elections.aspx	877/767-6446 614/466-2585

Oklahoma	State Election Board, Oklahoma City, OK	http://www.ok.gov/elections	405/521-2391
Oregon	Elections Division, Office of the Secretary of State, Salem, OR	http://sos.oregon.gov/voting-elections/Pages/default.aspx	503/986-1518
Pennsylvania	Bureau of Commissions, Elections and Legislation, Department of State, Harrisburg, PA	http://www.dos.pa.gov/VotingElections/Pages/default.aspx#.V1g-bTUrKmw	717/787-5280
Puerto Rico	State Elections Commission	http://ceepur.org	787/777-8682
Rhode Island (Candidates on Ballot)	Elections Division, Office of the Secretary of State, Providence, RI	http://www.sos.ri.gov/elections	401/222-2340
Rhode Island (Election Results)	State Board of Elections, Providence, RI	http://www.elections.ri.gov	401/222-2345
South Carolina	State Election Commission, Columbia, SC	http://www.scvotes.org	803/734-9060
South Dakota	Office of the Secretary of State, Pierre, SD	https://sdsos.gov/elections-voting/default.aspx	605/773-3537

State	Office	Website	Phone
Tennessee	Elections Division, Office of the Secretary of State, Nashville, TN	http://sos.tn.gov/elections	615/741-7956
Texas	Elections Division, Office of the Secretary of State, Austin, TX	http://www.sos.state.tx.us/elections/index.shtml	800/252-8683 512/463-5650
Utah	Elections Office, Office of the Lieutenant Governor, Salt Lake City, UT	http://www.elections.utah.gov	800/995-8683 801/538-1041
Vermont	Office of the Secretary of State, Montpelier, VT	https://www.sec.state.vt.us/elections.aspx	802/828-2363
Virginia	State Board of Elections, Richmond, VA	http://elections.virginia.gov/	800/552-9745 804/864-8901
U.S. Virgin Islands	Office of the Supervisor of Elections, St. Croix, USVI	http://www.vivote.gov	340-773-1021
Washington	Elections Division, Office of the Secretary of State, Olympia, WA	http://www.sos.wa.gov/elections	800/448-4881 360/902-4180

West Virginia	Office of the Secretary of State, Charleston, WV	http://www.sos.wv.gov/elections/Pages/default.aspx	866/767-8683 304/558-6000
Wisconsin	Government Accountability Board, Madison, WI	http://gab.wi.gov	608/266-8005
Wyoming	Office of the Secretary of State, Cheyenne, WY	http://soswy.state.wy.us/Elections/Elections.aspx	307/777-5860

Note: Every two years, the Commission publishes <u>Federal Elections,</u> a compilation of the official, certified federal election results obtained from each state's election office and other official sources. For a complete directory of the state offices that disclose campaign finance and election data, please see the Commission's *Combined Federal/ State Disclosure and Election Directory.*